D1293495

WAR WITHOUT GUNS

AMERICAN CIVILIANS IN RURAL VIETNAM

WAR WITHOUT GUNS

AMERICAN CIVILIANS IN RURAL VIETNAM

George K. Tanham

With

W. Robert Warne, Earl J. Young,
and William A. Nighswonger

FREDERICK A. PRAEGER, Publishers

New York · Washington · London

FREDERICK A. PRAEGER, PUBLISHERS
111 Fourth Avenue, New York, N.Y. 10003, U.S.A.
77–79 Charlotte Street, London, W.1, England

Published in the United States of America in 1966
by Frederick A. Praeger, Inc., Publishers

Library of Congress Catalog Card Number: 66-13671

Printed in the United States of America

This book is dedicated
to all the members of the Office of Provincial Operations,
to the many devoted Vietnamese with whom we worked,
and to Joseph Grainger,
Provincial Representative in Phu Yen Province,
who gave his life while on duty in Vietnam

PREFACE

IN THE PROVINCES of Vietnam, the Communist Viet Cong have been waging a revolution while the Government of Vietnam and the United States have been primarily fighting a war. In the towns and cities, as well as in the rural areas, there is ferment and a sense of dissatisfaction—the symptoms of a semilatent revolution. Independent of Communist activities, this Vietnamese revolution is groping for an ethos, for viable political institutions, and for social and economic improvements.[1] The Viet Cong have used this dissatisfaction and desire for change to build their own organization and influence. They want not only to encourage the revolution they see developing in the rural areas, but also to control that revolution and incorporate their own goals into it so as eventually to effect a Communist state. The United States and the Government of Vietnam have had more limited objectives.

The overt Viet Cong goals have been constantly expounded and are simple and understandable. They are intended to appeal to the peasant. The Viet Cong want to drive the United States "imperialists," who bomb and napalm the people, from

[1] See George Carver, "The Real Revolution in South Vietnam," *Foreign Affairs*, XLIII, No. 3 (April, 1965), 387, 408.

Vietnam. They want to overthrow the Saigon government, which, they say, does not represent the people and is a tool of the imperialists. They want "honest" efficient government and an end to the corruption and bumbling of officials from top to bottom. They wish to get rid of the landlords who get rich from the peasants' labor and to give the peasant land. In general, they focus on the local immediate needs of the peasant and promise redress from all wrongs and a better way of life. They feed on the fact that the Saigon government promises much but does little.

While the Communists appear willing to settle for an interim neutralist coalition in Saigon, they have made it clear that their real objective is the acquisition of total power. A coalition government would be only a step toward the ultimate formation of a wholly Communist government and unification with the Communist government of Hanoi. When that occurs, no political parties other than the Communist will be permitted and there will be no competing political entities. The stern dictatorship of the Communist Party will determine policies and procedures for the government. The basic freedoms of speech, press, and assembly, as well as free elections, which the West regards as essential not only to democracy but also to the dignity of man, will not be allowed to develop. One of the Western world's greatest contributions to civilization, the entire set of political principles and ideals clearly enunciated in the U.S. Declaration of Independence and the French Declaration of the Rights of Man, will not be available to this area.[2]

Once the major goal—the acquisition of political power—is attained, the Viet Cong plan to implement their real goals,

---

[2] This is not to suggest that the Vietnamese should adopt American or Western institutions and procedures. They must develop their own, but they should be exposed to and have the benefit of general concepts and principles developed during the past centuries. It is ironic that Ho Chi Minh, in his Declaration of Independence in 1946, quoted approvingly from the American Declaration of Independence.

not now publicized, and to make basic changes in all aspects of life. Free enterprise and private ownership of land will be abolished. While the concept of free enterprise may not be strong in Vietnam, most peasants want and hope to own their own land and to be secure on it. The Communists hold out land to the peasant now, but in the long run he will be deprived of it under a Communist regime. The collectivization programs in the two most viable Communist nations—the Soviet Union and China—would clearly be the models for Vietnam. The class structure will also be forcibly changed. Religion and other competing ideologies and institutions will be persecuted and eventually abolished. Thus the society, culture, and economy will be radically changed to conform to Communist requirements. However, these narrowly Communistic goals are not stressed to the peasants at this stage of the revolutionary war.

While the Viet Cong have exploited rural dissatisfaction, the governments of South Vietnam from Diem to the present have not met this challenge with constructive attempts to eradicate these long-standing ills. Nor have they been able to develop a Vietnamese national ideology or formulate a national program that could serve to unite the people, provide the basis for responsible and effective government, and show the way toward real economic and social progress. In spite of frequent high-sounding government declarations, there has been no real revolutionary effort. There is a desperate need for a Vietnamese "New Deal" with a definite program and psychological appeal. Furthermore, the various Saigon governments, except for Diem's, have not shown that they can govern or control the people, and none has shown itself capable of winning the long-term loyalty of the people. However, Premier Ky appears to be providing governmental stability in Saigon and is attempting to bring about social and political reform and greater rural development. It is too early to make any judgments on the progress of this program.

An imaginative, determined government could institute some programs that would have quick impact on the people. Land reform (often not redistribution, but merely better rental and interest rates and improvements in tenure systems), an efficient system of justice, an effective grievance program, an appealing and constructive program for Viet Cong defectors, price support for rice and ceilings on other costs are among the foremost measures needed. In the past, as will be shown, lack of interest, urban orientation, desire for personal gain, and inadequate numbers of trained civil servants have been some of the main blocks to such actions.

The goals of the United States, as an ally of the Vietnamese, are of necessity more general than those of the Government of Vietnam and the Viet Cong. President Johnson in his address at Johns Hopkins, on April 7, 1965, stated the overall United States objective in Vietnam. He said we want an independent nation, secure from attack and free to seek its own destiny in its own fashion. To achieve this goal, the United States has become increasingly involved in Vietnamese affairs. Since the establishment of an independent Vietnam in 1954, the United States has had a Military Assistance Advisory Group, a foreign-aid mission (now under the auspices of the Agency for International Development), and a United States Information Service Office in the country. Over the years, these missions have increased in size and in the scope of their work, and in addition there are now about 200,000 United States combat troops. At first, the United States advised primarily on military and economic matters, and restricted its activities largely to Saigon. Today there are military advisers from the battalion level of the Vietnamese Army up to corps level,[3] as well as with the Vietnamese Joint General Staff in Saigon and at the province and district levels of

---

[3] For military purposes, South Vietnam is divided into four corps areas. See map on p. 2. The corps areas are essentially military headquarters with few civilian responsibilities.

the government. Civilians advise in Saigon, at corps level, and in the provinces. United States advice covers the whole range of activities from military and economic to social and psychological, and the United States Embassy urges and exhorts in the political field. The cost of this effort is several million dollars a day.

In order to achieve its general goal, the United States has become involved very deeply in the life of Vietnam. To remain independent and free to choose its own destiny, Vietnam must have a stable and effective government and a viable economic system and social structure. Without these, the Communists could more easily take over and freedom of choice would disappear. The United States, by means of its Agency for International Development mission (called, in Vietnam, the United States Operations Mission, or USOM), has attempted through advice and help in public administration to improve the government; through advice and money in the public-works, agricultural, and industrial fields to develop the economy; and through aid to education and health to improve certain areas in the social field.

This book is about one small but important part of this United States advisory and assistance effort in Vietnam—the work of the Office of Provincial Operations (originally called the Office of Rural Affairs),[4] which is a part of the United States Operations Mission. This book does not attempt to provide a history of this office or details on all its operations. It is concerned rather with the life and work of the civilian American advisers in three provinces, one from each of the three major geographical subdivisions of Vietnam. This is the "war without guns" being waged by men of good will half a world away from their native land.

The introductory chapter outlines the problems facing the

[4] The Office of Provincial Operations included slightly more than 100 men, or about 1/250 of the total United States military and civilian advisory effort as of the summer of 1965.

Government of Vietnam and the United States in Vietnam and describes briefly the response to these problems, including the organization in 1962 of a stronger rural effort by both the Government of Vietnam and the United States. It traces the origin, mission, and organizational problems of the Office of Provincial Operations. In Chapter 2, Robert Warne writes about Vinh Binh Province, in the Mekong Delta, and his work and life there with his wife and young daughter. Chapter 3, by Earl Young, deals with Phu Bon Province, in the High Plateau area. In Chapter 4, William Nighswonger describes Quang Nam, a central coastal province in which the United States air base at Da Nang is located, and his work and life there. The last chapter attempts to evaluate the work of the Office of Provincial Operations, to suggest improvements, and to highlight and summarize the difficulties and dilemmas facing the United States in rural Vietnam.

The heart of this rural effort in Vietnam on the American side is the Provincial Representative. He is an American civilian who works full time in the provinces, usually lives in Vietnamese houses, and eats Vietnamese food. He gets to know the Vietnamese peasants. He travels around his province—usually unarmed—spurring on the local officials and trying to help them do their job better. Every single Provincial Representative has been shot at or ambushed, several have been wounded, and one has given his life. They are highly motivated Americans who daily risk their lives to contribute to American goals in Vietnam and to help the Vietnamese people. Three of them have contributed chapters to this book, writing really in the place of all their colleagues, any of whom could write a book about his experiences. This book focuses chiefly on the American effort, but we are only the advisers; the Vietnamese must be the doers if Vietnam is to become a viable nation.

It is the hope of the authors of this book that it will contribute to a better understanding of Vietnam and of the problems that nation and its ally, the United States, face. The authors wish also to demonstrate that the United States has tried, down to the grass roots, to help the Vietnamese build a nation, a viable economy, and a healthy society; that United States aid and support to Vietnam have not been solely military. Furthermore, if in the future, the Government of Vietnam and the United States achieve a military victory, this kind of program will be essential for a lasting peace in Vietnam.

The views and opinions expressed in this book are those of the authors and do not necessarily reflect those of the organizations and government agencies with which they are associated. No effort has been made to reconcile any differences among the contributors, since experiences in the various provinces often can lead one to different views and conclusions. Indeed, it is our hope that this book will contribute to a better understanding of the diversity of this small country.

—GEORGE K. TANHAM

CONTENTS

ILLUSTRATIONS

WAR WITHOUT GUNS

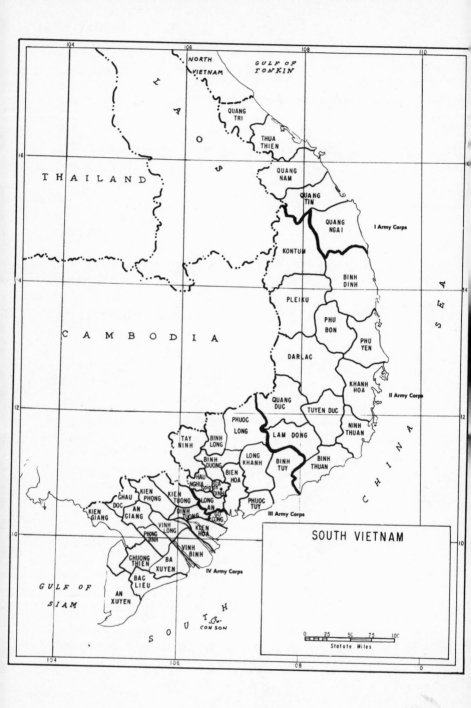

I

CHALLENGE AND RESPONSE

THERE ARE FORTY-THREE provinces in Vietnam, no two precisely the same in size, population, ethnic composition, climate, or any of a host of other aspects. They range from about 50,000 people in Phu Bon to nearly 1 million people in Binh Dinh and the few large provinces. Some provinces are mountainous with a vast majority of their inhabitants being *montagnards* (mountain people) of varying non-Vietnamese ethnic backgrounds. They are an extremely primitive, seminomadic group with languages, customs, and social and economic practices quite different from those of the Vietnamese. Like most highlanders throughout the world, they do not like the lowlanders, the Vietnamese in this case, and this dislike is reciprocated by the Vietnamese, who look down on the backward *montagnards*. The Mekong Delta provinces are flat and partially under water during the monsoon period, and several have a Cambodian ethnic minority. A few have strong elements of military-politico-religious sects, which were neutralized under Diem's government but which have come into the open since his overthrow, in 1963. Tay Ninh is the center of the Cao Dai sect, while the southwestern provinces have a number of Hoa Hao adherents. Many of the coastal provinces rely heavily on fishing for a living, while most of the others concentrate on rice, and a few, such as Binh Duong, Long Khanh, and Lam Dong, have large rubber and tea plantations. Certain older areas, around the city of Hué, for instance, have a strong regional tradition that gives them an identity distinct from the rest of Vietnam. The Delta provinces, on the other hand, were settled in the last few centuries and do not have this rich heritage. All these differences and peculiarities make the problems of development and counterinsurgency difficult and complex.

The province is the echelon immediately below the central government and a key one in the present struggle. In some ways, a province can be likened to one of the states of the United States, except that Vietnam has a unitary government. All power resides in Saigon, which may, however, delegate responsibilities in the provinces. The Province Chief, usually a political appointee and now in almost every case a military man, has several jobs and bosses. As a soldier, he is the sector commander in charge of the Regional and Popular Forces (local troops less well trained and equipped than the regular army) and is generally responsible to the division and corps commanders over him. He is also the senior civil administrator in the province, responsible to the Minister of Interior, and as such, he controls certain monies and civil servants. He is also coordinator of the activities of personnel from other ministries, such as Public Works, Health, and Education. These officials do not work for him directly, but for their ministries, so his control and influence vary, depending on his ability and their willingness to cooperate.

The Province Chief also supervises the District Chiefs under him and, in a general way, the Village Chiefs. There are from three to a dozen districts within a province. The district administration, consisting of an appointed District Chief and a small staff, is really only an arm of the province administration. Within a district, there are a number of villages, which are the lowest unit of government. The Village Chief customarily is elected and, together with the village council, runs local affairs. Because of the present emergency, most Village Chiefs are now appointed by the Province Chief. A village generally sprawls over a considerable area, and the population clusters within it are defined as hamlets—from two or three to perhaps eight or nine in each village. The insurgency has brought some status to the hamlet, which traditionally has not been an echelon of government. Since the villages are too spread out to be defended effectively, the hamlet was selected as the unit of defense in Diem's efforts to provide security for the rural people. These fortified hamlets were to make up the projected Strategic Hamlet Program.

At the top of the administrative pyramid is the Saigon government, which, like many other governments in Asia and elsewhere in the world for that matter, tends to be urban-oriented and inadequately responsive to rural needs. This is quite natural for a variety of reasons. Since cities and towns have more, and higher-level, schools, most of the educated people are found in the cities, and they prefer to stay in them. Wealth tends to be concentrated in a few cities whose residents thereby have access to higher education abroad. In addition, the rich cities constitute a power lever within the country. The best jobs in the government and in business are in the cities, so opportunity lies there. Entertainment and all the other attractions of city life exert additional drawing power. There is, therefore, a self-perpetuating power elite, which, although it may be "crashed" by the able country boy, dominates the entire life of the country. This elite tends to look down on the rural population, to distrust and dislike it, and to be unconcerned about its welfare or interests.

During seventy years of rule, the French did not develop among the Vietnamese a capacity for government; nor did they encourage professional training.[1] To some extent, they actually

---

[1] The British appear to have been much better at educating and training the Malayans. The civil servants and police in Malaya were key factors in the success against the terrorists in the post-World War II period.

reinforced the mandarin approach to government and life. After the arrival of the French, the few Vietnamese who were French-educated often became culturally split personalities— as much French as Vietnamese. For example, even though Diem disliked the French because of their opposition to Vietnamese nationalism, he often carried on official Vietnamese business in French. This cultural orientation tended to widen the gulf between the government and the masses, especially in the countryside. The concentration of power, influence, and education in an urban few did not prepare the country for independence in 1954, nor did it lay the groundwork for responsible and responsive government for the masses.

Before the French takeover in the late nineteenth century, Vietnam was ruled by an emperor residing in Hué. The administration of the country was in the hands of the mandarins chosen on the basis of intellectual achievement. These men, appointed and removed by the emperor, were the real local rulers of Vietnam, and opposed all change. There was little local participation in government and few opportunities for advancement. Given this background, and the more recent Diem dictatorship, the Vietnamese have not yet developed many mature political leaders who could rally the people and provide effective government attuned to their needs. There is also a dearth of trained and dedicated civil servants to carry on the day-to-day administration of government at the Saigon level and below. For example, there is a real shortage of budget personnel, and the police force is understaffed and ill trained. A judicial system is almost nonexistent. Thus, even in the urban areas, government is spotty and inadequate while in many of the rural areas it is often corrupt or totally absent.

The Saigon government's lack of interest in and disdain for the rural population and the shortage of trained government officials have greatly facilitated the Communists' task. Generally, the most incompetent officials have been sent into the provinces. Since advancement in careers and economic opportunities lies in Saigon, the best men refuse to go into the provinces. Many of the officials in the rural areas are, therefore, bitter at having to vegetate far from the hub of affairs, and they have little or no feeling for the people or their needs and aspirations.

Until 1962, the United States contributed to the perpetuation of this urban bias.[2] Few Americans went out into the countryside to help the Government of Vietnam to ascertain the character of the peasants' problems and needs, or to develop programs to assist in rural nation-building. The emphasis was on long-term large-scale projects, such as the highway connecting Bien Hoa and Saigon, which had little impact on the rural areas. The civilians, like the military, thought along conventional lines and proceeded in a leisurely fashion.

There are thus two problems facing the Government of Vietnam and its ally, the United States. First, this underdeveloped government must grapple with the broad spectrum of problems of an underdeveloped country. In Vietnam, there is plenty of food, though the diet is unbalanced and lacks protein. There are serious, almost overwhelming, health problems and great educational needs. There are economic problems: maldistribution of goods, too little diversification of the economy, and inadequate credit facilities. But besides these obvious needs are those nonmaterial ones so much more difficult to cope with—the development of a national bond with the Saigon government, satisfaction of growing desires for social and political institutions to match the modern material order being created, and responsible and intelligent leadership at all echelons of government and society.

There is the second, and at the moment critical, problem of a dedicated and well-organized group that uses these many is-

[2] In 1954–55, handling of refugees did take Americans into the countryside, where much excellent resettlement and rehabilitation work was done, but once that operation was terminated, it was not until 1962 that Americans in any numbers went into the rural area for long periods.

sues to attack the government and replace it with its own apparatus. The Viet Cong claim to be promoting the welfare of the people, and they make much of the government's failures in the political, social, and economic fields. However, they reveal their real goals by opposing measures to improve the people's well-being when it appears that this may hurt their own cause. For example, the malaria-eradication program, which has been quite successful in its effects on health and its psychological impact, has been opposed in many instances by the Viet Cong; they have killed malaria workers and have spread the charge that the spraying is bad for the people. In other cases, they opposed the building of fish ponds, which were to be stocked with Tilapia fish to increase the protein in the peasants' diet, and said the fish were poisonous. They destroyed schools. They killed officials who were trying to help the people, and they interfered with measures designed to improve material aspects of life. The Government of Vietnam thus has a rival for power which uses dissatisfaction of the people as a support, but which often opposes solutions to these problems in order to weaken the government.

These two problem areas are related but separate. Economic improvement, social progress, and the creation of responsible democratic government, though they may go far toward solving the problems of an underdeveloped country, will not necessarily defeat the Viet Cong. The Communist military and political organization or infrastructure must be smashed before that problem is solved. What may be necessary to defeat the Communist threat—an effective police force, a large army, population and resource controls—is not necessarily the best means for combating the problems of underdevelopment. These problems demand skilled manpower and resources and money to wage the struggle for progress. However, development programs may, at the same time, demonstrate that the government can govern and will prevail. Both the military threat and the broad-spectrum problems of underdevelopment involve dilemmas and hard decisions and there are no quick and easy short cuts.

Many Vietnamese nationalists saw World War II as an opportunity to gain independence from France. Some of the moderates envisaged an autonomous Vietnam within the French Union, while others wished Vietnam to be completely independent. During the war, Ho Chi Minh, a nationalist and a Communist, founded the Vietnam Doc Lap Dong Minh Hoi (Vietnam Independence League), more commonly known as the Vietminh, which was intended to coordinate all efforts for a free Vietnam. Besides Ho Chi Minh, the leadership included other Communists, such as Vo Nguyen Giap (now Vice Premier and Minister of Defense of North Vietnam) and Pham Van Dong (now Prime Minister of North Vietnam), as well as many non-Communist nationalists. Much, but by no means all, of the membership came from the old Indochinese Communist Party. During the war, the Vietminh organized in the villages and began to develop guerrilla forces to fight the French and Japanese. By the end of the war, the Vietminh guerrilla troops and organization were the strongest national force in Vietnam. After the war, the Communist leadership, trying to rally all Vietnamese nationalists around the Vietminh banner, de-emphasized the Communist aspects and goals. Ngo Dinh Diem was one of the nationalist leaders who refused to cooperate with the Vietminh.

The Vietminh proclaimed Vietnamese independence in 1945, and discussions were then held between Ho Chi Minh and the French on the future of Vietnam. These negotiations failed, and all hope for a peaceful agreement was lost when the Vietminh attacked the French forces in the Red River Delta in December, 1946. The Vietminh were nearly crushed but their leadership survived along with some of the cadres, and these remnants began the eight-year war against the

French. They started as weak guerrillas, but ultimately developed into a powerful organization with seven regular line divisions and an independent governmental structure.

The long but successful struggle of the Vietminh against the French, which culminated at Dien Bien Phu in May, 1954, led to peace talks in Geneva. In July, 1954, the Geneva Accords, an armistice providing for the division of Vietnam along the 17th parallel, were signed. This dividing line was considered temporary, as the Accords also called for nationwide elections in July, 1956. Furthermore, the Accords provided that, if they wished, civilians on either side of this essentially military dividing line could move to the other zone within 300 days. Nearly 1 million Northerners, largely Catholics, came South, while well over 100,000 Southerners went North. Not all of the Southern Communists, however, went North. Many stayed in the South; some clandestinely continued their Vietminh activities, while others forgot the war and the Vietminh and tried to settle down to a normal life. In the South, the major concentrations of Vietminh power and influence were in the Camau Peninsula, the Plain of Reeds, Zone D, and a coastal area overlapping parts of Quang Ngai and Binh Dinh. There were many smaller, less secure areas that the Communists also utilized to maintain their movement after the armistice. The Communists, in both the North and the South, expected victory in the scheduled elections in 1956.

By 1956, Diem had scored a surprising political success in the South. He had developed a stable government and defeated the sects (the Hoa Hao, Cao Dai, Binh Xuyen). He refused to hold the elections primarily because even if he had obtained all the votes in the South, which was doubtful, the more populous and more tightly administered North would have won the elections. This refusal changed the situation for the Communists and posed a new problem. They were forced to resort to revolutionary war instead of elections to gain power.

By the end of the 1950's, the Communist leadership in the South and in Hanoi believed that the situation was ripe for them to launch stronger overt action against the Diem government. They felt that their covert organization was ready to begin the struggle and that Diem's peasant support could be weakened. Assassinations of and attacks against local officials, teachers, and other key personnel became more numerous. It has been estimated that in 1959 about 1,700 such persons were assassinated; this figure rose to 4,000 in 1960. Furthermore, during 1960, these activities spread into new areas and military operations were begun.

In December, 1960, the establishment of the National Liberation Front was announced. Ostensibly a broad coalition, it announced a number of goals, among them, the unification of Vietnam. It recruited members from a number of non-Communist South Vietnamese groups, including the Buddhists and Catholics, and maintained an appearance of independence from Hanoi. The location of its headquarters was unknown and was probably moved often. In January, 1962, a purely Communist organization, the People's Revolutionary Party, was formed. This party had strong ties with, if it was not controlled by, the Dang Lao Dong—the Communist Party of North Vietnam. By filling key positions and having a tight organization, it dominated the National Liberation Front and propagated the Communist line. In March, 1962, the National Liberation Front held its first Congress, which, in order to maintain its independent appearance, elected a non-Communist Saigon lawyer, Nguyen Huu Tho, as President and Professor Nguyen Van Hieu to the key position of Secretary General. The Front is now essentially a shadow government, probably headquartered in the northern section of Tay Ninh Province. It has representatives in several foreign countries, including Cuba and Algeria, and increasingly presses its claims to be the rightful government of the people of South Vietnam. Thus, the Viet Cong now have an official party and a shadow government.[3] Both of these have representatives in almost all parts of the country. They have a hard-core army of 70,000 troops in battalion- and regimental-size units, 100,-000 guerrillas, and probably several million sympathizers.[4]

These developments followed the general principles of Mao Tse-tung and North Vietnamese General Vo Nguyen Giap, who preached that there are three major phases of a Communist revolution. The first is the covert political and organizational phase; the second begins when it is deemed time to launch guerrilla operations; and the third and final phase is almost conventional warfare, launched only when the political and military base is secure and other conditions propitious. Before the end of the war against the French, North Vietnam developed into phase three: the Vietminh had regular divisions and waged a more or less conventional war. The southern part of Vietnam never got past phase two, the guerrilla phase. Today in South Vietnam, certain areas are controlled and administered by the Viet Cong, and certain revolutionary changes are being attempted. In contrast, other areas have been more resistant to Viet Cong advances and may be only in the first phase or early in the second phase of the revolution. Even more important than possible geographic distinctions is the fact that the political and organizational activities of phase one never stop. In fact, it is probably more accurate to describe the phases as layers on a cake. The first layer is never removed, but the second is added to it, and the third if necessary. The Viet Cong continuously indoctrinate, organize, and manipulate the population. If the area is under their control, this is easier, can be done openly, and is carried to greater extremes. The Communists realize that in order to

[3] Viet Cong means Vietnamese Communist and is generally applied to the entire insurgent apparatus—both the civilian and the military elements. The term is so used in this book.

[4] In addition, it has been estimated that by the end of 1965 North Vietnam had infiltrated between two and three regular divisions into South Vietnam.

maintain permanent control, military victories are not enough. A political organization must exist that can control the people. The guerrillas of the second phase are added, but in phase three, when more conventional forces predominate, political action and guerrillas still play a role.

The present impressive and imposing insurgent apparatus is based on the earlier Vietminh organization. Its strength lies in the rural areas, where Viet Cong agents have worked hard for years. They have visited with the peasants in a village, gotten to know them, lived with them, and listened to them. They have learned about their grievances, their attitudes toward the various local officials and other important local people, and in many places, have been accepted as sympathetic persons who want to help the peasant. The traditional Vietnamese distrust and dislike of officials has been cleverly played upon so that the peasant finds himself criticizing the entire government as well as specific local officials. Real or imagined abuses or injustices have been exaggerated by the Viet Cong. It is easy to picture the absentee landlord who exacts high rents and high interest rates as a brutal oppressor. More recently, the Americans have been described as backers of the corrupt and hated officials and the greedy landlords and, furthermore, as profiteers on their own.

Until the November, 1963, coup, the Viet Cong agent, who is often originally a Vietnamese peasant himself and shares the life of the peasant, held out an alternative to the "corrupt and oppressive Diem government." In recent years, he offers a substitute for "American puppet governments"—the National Liberation Front, which, he says, is fighting for the people and is supported and recognized by many great nations throughout the world. The peasant is gradually enticed into helping the Front by providing a little food for some men who are "fighting the people's battle," helping with some of the portage problems, making traps to be used against government troops, and assisting in anti-government propaganda. Once involved, and guilty of working against his government, it is hard for him to disengage himself.

Meanwhile, other Viet Cong agents have infiltrated or expanded the infiltration of farmers' groups, women's associations, and especially youth organizations. Even religious institutions are used; Viet Cong instructions have been captured that urge greater participation in religious life because it is respected and influential and can be mobilized in behalf of the Communist effort.

This infiltration goes on not only in rural areas, but also in the cities, where the target is often the military and administrative offices of the government. Infiltration personnel in the urban areas must be more careful than the organizing agents in the rural areas because of more intimate contacts with the government and closer surveillance. But they can often skillfully spread Communist propaganda to government officials and the military. For example, in Saigon, they can remark that most of the big houses and big cars are occupied by Americans.

The organizing agent in the rural area continues to propagandize the peasants, to incite them against their government, and to become a leader who can help them redress certain injustices. He does not make appeals based on general ideas such as Communism, which would have little meaning for the average peasant, but concentrates on very real, very immediate, and by now very serious issues. Landlord X is very greedy, the Deputy District Chief is a notorious thief, and the local policeman is a crook and a pawn of the rich. The peasants understand and suffer these injustices, and they want to change them.

The agent continually sizes up the people of the village to determine which ones would be useful adherents to the cause, which ones are not worthy, and which ones will help but not join. Cells are organized for the youth, propaganda is intensified, and instructions in guerrilla warfare are begun for select young men. Some of these activities are carried on clandestinely in the village; in other cases, the youth leave and go to a Viet Cong base for training and indoctrination.

The Viet Cong are good organizers and realize the value of organizations with strict discipline. In villages gradually being drawn into the Viet Cong net, as well as in villages and camps already won by the Viet Cong, an inner political organization of trusted and dedicated members is developed. As the movement has progressed, so the organization has extended and grown. One writer has very perceptively stated that the Viet Cong organization is like a coral reef; it starts from the bottom but slowly and methodically builds up.[5] It is this basic organization and discipline which is one of the greatest strengths of the Viet Cong. An important point is that *before* terror or military action begins, the grass-roots political propaganda and organizational effort are initiated and developed to the point where the Viet Cong believe it wise to proceed to more overt action. In general, the Communists build carefully and do not move until they feel confident of success.

While the Communists always make much of winning the support of the people and insist that guerrillas must have popular support to be effective, they do not always use appeals and persuasion. Their instruction manuals do insist that troops and civilians treat the people well, help them, and give them propaganda talks. However, as their organization has grown, they have increasingly resorted to coercing, kipnaping, and pressing young peasants into the Viet Cong organization.

Terror as a weapon is usually, but not always, employed on a selective basis and designed to achieve a certain purpose. If there is a particularly unpopular and corrupt local official, the Viet Cong may decide to kill him in order to gain an image as the protector and defender of the people. There have been many cases in Vietnam when the slaying of certain officials

[5] Stanley Karnow, "This Is Our Enemy," *Saturday Evening Post*, August 22–29, 1964, p. 23.

was supported and cheered by the local population. However, no official, good or bad, is safe from Viet Cong attack. If he is a good official, the Viet Cong may threaten him several times and tell him to leave the area. If he does not do this (many do leave), they may kill him. The propaganda line will be that though he was good, he worked for a corrupt, dishonest, and imperialistic government. If there are several savage killings in an area, government officials may quit the area and essentially leave it to the Viet Cong, or it may become increasingly difficult to fill vacant positions. Other terrorist actions have as an objective the intimidation of the people so that they will refuse to assist their own government, and help the Viet Cong instead.

Terror is a two-edged weapon, and even with the most careful planning, it may backfire. What appears to us to be indiscriminate terror, such as the mining of school or civilian buses or the burning of all the houses in a village, may be deliberate actions to create a sense of fear and to show the impotence of the government; but it can also arouse the people against the Viet Cong. For example, the people have protested the killing of good officials and other acts of terror. At other times, the Viet Cong may be prevented from giving a propagandistic explanation for their terrorist acts, and therefore reap a loss rather than a gain. Whether the people's response is positive or negative, the over-all Communist objective of breaking down and paralyzing the government is usually aided by terrorist acts.

Because of the Viet Cong terror, the government is finding it hard to fill rural offices. It is virtually impossible to maintain government in certain areas. Sometimes there is a village government "in exile." The officials may go to their village in the daytime but retire to a safer village or town at night, or they may not be able to visit their village at all. Peasants, by nature not very generous with information, are in such circumstances even more taciturn and reluctant to provide information to government officials or the military. The inability of the government to protect the peasant or to govern in certain areas demonstrates its weakness and is making the peasants become neutrals if not supporters of the Viet Cong. While the Viet Cong may suffer from their excessive terror, they do not lose face as the legal government does when its feebleness is demonstrated. Furthermore, anarchy in any case helps the Viet Cong.

More than enough has been written on the military aspects of the Viet Cong in this conflict, so only a brief summary of the main points will be given here. Essentially, the tactics are those of the weak and poorly equipped. Ambushes, surprise attacks, night attacks, and attacks in overwhelming numbers are the usual form. Attacks against forts and villages are carefully planned and often rehearsed many times. The Viet Cong soldier tries to fight when and where he chooses. He always prepares a means of escape should the fighting go badly. He is afraid of air power and artillery, and tries to develop techniques to avoid them. He is primarily an infantry man who can walk long and far and lives simply and frugally. He skillfully uses mortars and recoilless weapons, as well as mines. Some of these weapons are homemade, many are American, and an increasing number come from Communist countries. All in all, the Viet Cong soldier is hard to beat on his own terms. Because he tries to avoid fighting on others' terms, methods must be devised to force him to fight when he doesn't want to.

Besides fighting, the Viet Cong soldier has other responsibilities that are continually emphasized to him in his daily training and indoctrination. The political purposes of the struggle always have priority. All actions, personal and group, are directed to these ends. The troops are instructed to treat the people courteously and with respect, to pay for what they take, and to assist them whenever possible. They are also supposed to explain to the people why they are fighting and to attempt to gain popular support. Thus, by word and deed the

Viet Cong soldier is intended to play an important role in the basic political and psychological struggle.

These high standards are not always met. Some Viet Cong do not pay for what they take, hurt the people, and neglect to help when they could. Their actions may also bring destruction and death to the villages. Sometimes they will fire at government aircraft and so bring on an air attack or artillery bombardment. This is done deliberately on occasions in order to turn the people against their government, which is then portrayed as hurting them. This often backfires, and the peasants are incensed when they recognize that the attack was brought on by Viet Cong actions. At other times, the Viet Cong burn up villages known to have cooperated with the government, seize hostages, carry off the youth, and mistreat the people. In one instance, they used the population of a village as a shield against the Vietnamese Army and forced the people to burn their own houses. This antagonized the villagers, but again demonstrated the impotence of the government. Many Americans in Vietnam believe that the Viet Cong are now relying much more heavily on force and terror to recruit and maintain their organization.[6]

Military actions, like terror and nonviolent means, are used to destroy and discredit the government so that a vacuum will exist which the Communists can fill. If this is accomplished by creating fear, rather than loyalty, in people's minds, this is quite acceptable to the Viet Cong.

Contrary to the Western conception of classical Communist doctrine, Communist military operations and tactics are usually directed toward politico-psychological goals, as well as toward military objectives. *The key to Communist strategy is the notion that all means—military, political, psychological, economic—must be orchestrated and channeled toward some po-*

[6] There is some evidence that Viet Cong terror—coupled with the inability to protect people in their areas from attack—is alienating many peasants, some of whom are fleeing to government-held areas.

litical goal on a day-to-day basis, not just at the peace table at the end of the struggle.

In the areas where these combined efforts have been successful, the Viet Cong establish their own village or district government, collect taxes and administer justice, and begin to initiate revolutionary social and economic measures. Land is taken from the landowners, many of whom are now in Saigon or other large cities, and redistributed to the peasants. While the peasant is led to believe, and apparently does believe, that he can keep this land, in the long run this will hardly be the case. He will probably have to surrender it to a state-run collective. Religious institutions are not tampered with, but the Communists develop and emphasize competing institutions to attract away women, youth, peasants, workers, and other groups. One of the striking aspects of the Communist-dominated areas is the high degree of organization of society and its mobilization in the Viet Cong cause.

While the Viet Cong do kidnap youth, employ terror, and are harsh at times with the people, they nevertheless clearly have appeal, especially for some of the young people. One possible explanation is that the latent and unarticulated psychological needs of the young are being met best by the Communists. In Vietnam, as in many other parts of the world, traditional institutions—the family, the village, the tribe, and religion—are disintegrating or at least seem unable to play a vital role for the young. Consequently, the loyalties and respect commanded by these institutions are reduced. Many of the young people feel rootless, unanchored, and restless. The more sensitive ones realize that the world is changing; movies and radios and other mass communications media constantly reveal this even in remote areas. The youth wonders what all this means to him, and perhaps even more importantly, how he can become a part of it. How, he asks, can he get an education, how can he get a responsible and respected position, and how can he share in the material benefits of modern life?

The village and his own government, which even at the provincial level is still rather remote, seem to offer few opportunities. The local officials' corruption and lack of interest do not encourage him. It is unlikely that he will obtain a high-school diploma, but without it, he cannot be a commissioned officer or an upper-level civil servant in his own government. If drafted into the army, he not only is destined to a career in the lowest ranks, but may be sent far from his local village into an unknown, strange, and essentially unmeaningful area, even if it is a part of Vietnam. His government does not seem to be a dynamic organization, with clear-cut goals that beckon him to serve and that satisfy some of his, perhaps unconscious, ambitions and needs.

The Viet Cong agent can work well with such people, who are often not aware of their own frustrations or needs, but know or feel that something is wrong and that life somehow can be better. The Viet Cong agent, who behaves properly and is sympathetic enough to listen, to spend time, and to encourage these youths, also offers them some alternatives. He talks about a movement whose goal is the improvement of the lot of the common people and which offers education and training.[7] Probably even more important, he offers an opportunity to belong to a new growing organization, with a future for all who are willing to work and serve. Why not, the agent suggests, come join our outfit, which fights for the country and against the rich and corrupt and the American imperialists who bomb the people? The hardships and dangers are minimized. To many young rural Vietnamese—flattered by an invitation to join—the siren call seems to promise

---

[7] The author has observed this phenomenon in other areas. In 1961, in northeast Thailand, he interviewed a number of persons who had been arrested by the Thai Government. He asked one man when he had become dissatisfied with the government, and the man replied: "June, 1959." When questioned further as to why it was so specific a time, he said: "A man told me I was unhappy with certain things and I suddenly realized he was right."

an opportunity to attain their ambitions, to do their duty, and to satisfy their cravings to belong. It is often too late when they realize that life with the Viet Cong is harsh and that the realities do not resemble the promises.

Although the Viet Cong do have appeal for some people, especially the young, and have developed an effective military and political organization, they do have serious weaknesses and problems. In the first place, they were forced, clandestinely in the beginning, to revise and expand the old Vietminh organization. They could not openly recruit, lacked finances, and could only promise opportunities and improvements. In addition to the other difficulties inherent in their covert status, they were illegal. While this point may seem only a technicality, it is important for the Viet Cong. They constantly strive for legality, perhaps for psychological reasons, but also for practical ones. Legality would give them a position in the world and an opportunity to be heard and to receive aid. Another problem is the slow and difficult logistics system within Vietnam and from North Vietnam. Some of the basic needs of life—food, clothes, and medical supplies—are in very short supply in the Viet Cong camp. Life is harsh and Spartan because of these shortages and the necessity to live the life of a fugitive. Many Viet Cong list this kind of life as the reason they quit or have low morale. As the size of the organization has increased, so have the problems of recruiting, discipline, and management. In fact, at this time, they seem to be having serious manpower problems, and there is evidence that women are now staffing some military units. Furthermore, in areas under their control, the Viet Cong face administrative problems, as well as the need to produce some of the things they have promised the people. The material things are hard to provide, although the Viet Cong do construct schools and other necessary buildings. Their form of justice is not always what the people expected, and taxes are increasingly high. Constructive

programs and positive government, the Viet Cong are dis-
covering, are more difficult to achieve than destruction and
criticism.

In the military field, the Viet Cong lack modern weapons,
although they receive some assistance from the North. They
do not have artillery or heavy equipment, but to a certain extent, this might be a burden rather than an asset to a force as
mobile as they are. They lack aircraft and suffer seriously from
the fact that the Government of Vietnam and the United
States have an abundance of both artillery and aircraft. The
Viet Cong are not able to protect villagers under their control
from Government and United States air attacks and are having
increasing difficulty in defending themselves against aggressive
ground actions. At the end of 1964, it appeared that this superiority was preventing the Viet Cong from proceeding to larger-
scale offensive operations of their own and might force the Viet
Cong back to a lower level of violence.

Generally, the Viet Cong buildup during the late 1950's
went unnoticed, or at best, its significance was inadequately
assessed. But by 1961, President Diem, and even more his
brother Counselor Nhu, recognized the Viet Cong activities
in the rural areas as a threat to their political base. Diem
claimed even before 1961 to have been concerned about the
guerrilla threat, but he had taken few measures to cope with
it and had been unsuccessful in enlisting United States support for counterinsurgency efforts. As the situation worsened
in 1961, Nhu realized that something had to be done. Being
politically acute, he realized that he must organize the people.
Partially as the result of advice from Sir Robert Thompson,
then head of the British Advisory Mission, and others, and
partially because of his awareness of the threat, Nhu initiated
the Strategic Hamlet Program. This program aimed at providing security for the rural population by moving them when
necessary to more compact clusters and constructing ditches

and barbed-wire fences as protection. It also aimed at separating the Viet Cong from their base—the people—and thus stopping the flow of goods and food to the insurgents. There were also supposed to be social and economic improvements and responsible political organizations in the hamlets, so that the people would be willing and able not only to defend themselves but to participate actively and loyally in developing a viable and Communist-resistant society.

Unfortunately, the program was pushed too fast and without regard for the people's feelings or real needs. Peasants were forcibly and abruptly moved and were made to build defenses, often without compensation. They enjoyed few tangible improvements as a result of these hardships and labor; the follow-up programs for social, economic, and political improvements rarely materialized. Hamlets were deemed completed when fortifications were finished, hardly the criterion for real pacification and progress. Communist propaganda to the effect that the strategic hamlets were really concentration camps often fell on very fertile ground.

As the situation worsened and Diem's concern intensified, the United States became increasingly aware of the growing Viet Cong threat and reacted in a number of ways. In the spring of 1961, Vice President Johnson made an official visit to Vietnam; in the summer, the government sent an economic mission headed by Eugene Staley, and in the autumn the Maxwell Taylor–W.W. Rostow mission was dispatched to evaluate the entire situation. Both these missions recommended additional military and nonmilitary assistance and more U.S. advisers. They suggested a reorientation of the U.S. effort: more attention to unconventional warfare and more counter-insurgency-oriented civil programs, and a reduction in the long-term economic development effort. There was some sense of urgency, and U.S. efforts were, in fact, accelerated as well as increased.

In the United States Operations Mission (USOM), William Fippin, first Assistant Director for Rural Affairs (with no staff) and later Acting Director, urged greater efforts in the countryside, and more attention to the insurgency. He established a Counterinsurgency Committee whose purpose was to formulate and coordinate an economic and social program as a complement to the increased military effort. Some of the initial projects included a police radio for each village, increased assistance to the *montagnards*, and improved agricultural methods. By no means did all the members of USOM agree to this reorientation, but by the spring of 1962, there were the beginnings of the switch to counterinsurgency projects.

In June, 1962, Rùfus Phillips, who had served as an Army adviser in Vietnam and also in Laos, was sent by AID to Vietnam to make general recommendations in the area of counterinsurgency. Phillips recognized that although Diem and Nhu and a few of the top Ministers were aware of the rural problem, most of the government officials were very negative, uninformed, and unresponsive to this increasingly critical problem. In view of the nature of the Saigon government and the attitudes of most officials, Phillips recommended that there be a decentralization of authority and money to the provincial levels on both the Government of Vietnam and U.S. sides. He also noted that the local provincial resources were very limited and that the central government had to assist quickly and efficiently if the Strategic Hamlet Program was to be successful. In order to prime the operations in the provinces, he urged that the U.S. purchase piasters that would be sent to and used in the provinces, thus circumventing the slow-moving Government of Vietnam ministries. Furthermore, he saw the need to provide a political basis that would serve to give the people a stake in their communities and ultimately in their government.

Phillips also suggested a new organization within the USOM that would have the responsibility for coordinating the AID counterinsurgency effort in the countryside. There would be

an Assistant Director for Rural Affairs with a small staff in
Saigon to deal with the appropriate Government of Vietnam
agencies in Saigon, particularly the Central Pacification Committee, headed by Counselor Nhu. A major innovation was
the proposal to establish the position of an AID Provincial
Representative in each province. These men would serve as
advisers to the Province Chief and his staff, would help ac-
celerate the rural programs, and would have funds and materials directly available. It was not intended that the Provincial
Representatives would replace the regular USOM technicians
from the health, education, agriculture, and public-works divisions; they would merely supplement them. None of these
technicians stayed in the provinces permanently, so the Provincial Representatives would supervise in a general way all
the social and economic work in the provinces on a continuing
daily basis.

By the summer of 1962, therefore, there was a strong move
to reorient the AID program to achieve three general objectives: (1) to reduce the interval between the time a counterinsurgency need develops in a province and the time commodities and services are delivered; (2) to decentralize authority,
funds, and personnel to the province level on the part of
USOM and, hopefully, on the part of the Government of
Vietnam, as well; (3) to provide flexibility to permit on-the-
spot changes and adaptations in the program as required by
the conflict. To achieve the first objective, administrative procedures, supply systems, and planning were modified. The second objective was sought by creating a new organization
within USOM—an Office for Rural Affairs, which would have
its own funds and personnel, all directed toward the countryside. The final goal was pursued partially through decentralization and partially through simplifying administrative procedures. It was hoped that this streamlining and decentralization
would permit the Government of Vietnam to come to grips
more quickly and effectively with the threat in the rural areas.

In September of 1962, Rufus Phillips returned to Vietnam as the first head of the Office of Rural Affairs and brought with him as his Deputy Albert Fraleigh, a seasoned AID official. Since the objective of the new office was to help produce immediate impact on the peasants, Phillips plunged into his work at once. Special arrangements for faster aid to the provinces, called Provincial Rehabilitation Agreements, were drawn up and agreed to by the Government of Vietnam and the United States. These agreements outlined general goals and implementation procedures. Special funds were earmarked for provincial rehabilitation by the Saigon government, and the United States purchased $10 million worth of piasters, which were allocated directly to the provinces. A Provincial Rehabilitation Committee was established in each province with the Province Chief as Chairman and the U.S. Military Sector Adviser and the U.S. Provincial Representative as members. The committee approved specific projects to be undertaken and established priorities. Though the Province Chief was the executive and made the decisions in the final analysis, the Americans had to countersign all expenditures of money. It was hoped that this machinery would speed and improve the pacification effort going on in the provinces.

In mid-1964, the name of the administering office was changed from Rural Affairs to Provincial Operations, but the over-all structure of the program remained the same. The goal was to have a Provincial Representative and an Assistant Provincial Representative in each of the forty-three provinces and two representatives at each of the four corps headquarters—a total of about a hundred men in the field.[8] However, at this writing, all these positions have not been filled. Hard-driving, imaginative, dedicated men are being sought from all walks of life. The United States Army and the State Department have loaned a few of their men for this effort; others have been re-

[8] Provincial Operations was also assisted by a Filipino contingent, about twenty of whom served in the provinces as Assistant Provincial Representatives.

cruited from retired military personnel, from other AID missions and other agencies of the government, as well as from private life. The Saigon office remains rather small; it consists of the Assistant Director and his Deputy, plus liaison officers with the Central Pacification Committee and the Ministry of Social Welfare, backstop officers for the Provincial Representatives, and a small administrative staff. The budget for the office has ranged around $60–$70 million a year.

The over-all mission of the Office of Provincial Operations has remained essentially unchanged since its inception. It is to advise and assist the Government of Vietnam, at the central and local levels, on the broad range of counterinsurgency efforts, particularly in connection with economic, social, and political development. The fundamental objectives are to aid the Government of Vietnam to develop the rural population into a Communist-resistant force and, working together with the local Vietnamese officials, to improve living conditions and to provide greater hope for the future. These objectives are largely based on the assumption that improved material welfare will make the people more loyal to their government.

The Office of Provincial Operations, in support of and together with the Government of Vietnam, has planned and is implementing a variety of programs aimed at achieving these objectives. In pursuit of improved security and administrative viability, the Provincial Rehabilitation Program is under way in each province. In concert with the Military Assistance Program, funds and material are provided to help the rural population construct fortifications for the hamlets and to organize for defense. In addition to training and advising local officials, administrative teams (cadres) have been organized and trained to bolster and improve the village governments. These activities, which are programed in the Provincial Rehabilitation Agreements, are planned in the province, sent to Saigon for approval, and implemented in the province with cash funds and other resources delivered in advance. The work is carried out under the general direction of the Provincial Committee. This decentralized system of program planning and execution assures a more realistic understanding of genuine local needs and a more timely and meaningful response to these needs. If correctly administered, this system may develop a closer and more harmonious relationship between the government and the rural population.

In addition to its Provincial Rehabilitation activities, the Office of Provincial Operations assists the provinces in responding to emergencies in strategic hamlets caused by natural disasters or by Viet Cong activities. Food, clothing, agricultural tools, and other commodities are shipped to hamlets or to refugee camps with all possible speed in order to demonstrate to the people the desire and ability of the government to assist them in a time of urgent need. Again, these activities are carried on through the facilities of the local administration under the direction of the Provincial Committee.

The Office of Provincial Operations, along with technicians from USOM, also supports and advises the Vietnamese on a wide range of economic and social programs. Some of these are carried out by provincial officials in cooperation with the regular Government of Vietnam ministries. A pig-corn program to improve the breed of hogs, a fertilizer and improved-seed effort to increase rice production, and a tree-planting effort to produce wood products are carried out in cooperation with the Ministry of Rural Affairs (the equivalent of the Department of Agriculture in the United States). Health activities, such as construction of surgical suites, dispensaries, and medical stations, are coordinated with the Ministry of Health. Other programs are planned and carried out by the provincial officials without assistance from Saigon ministries. These include small-scale local public works, such as the construction of market places and village roads and bridges. A third category are the so-called self-help projects. Ideally, these should be requested by the villagers and approved at the provincial level; in practice, they are often thrust upon the people by the province officials. In these self-help agreements the villagers agree to supply the labor, and the province provides money and materials. Under this program construction of schools, fish ponds, markets, and other small structures has been undertaken. This concept is new to Vietnam and it has not always worked well, though when the officials understand and approve of it, there have been some real successes.

Early in 1963, the Government of Vietnam launched the Chieu Hoi (Open-Arms) Program, designed to attract and rehabilitate Viet Cong defectors. This program was patterned after the successful experiment conducted by Ramón Magsaysay, the late Philippine President, against the Hukbalahap insurgents in the 1950's. Initially, Provincial Operations was assigned the advisory responsibility for Chieu Hoi. However, it soon became clear that the complexity of the program's approaches would involve not only the United States Operations Mission, but the United States Information Service, to assist with the propaganda aspects, and Military Assistance Command—Vietnam, to help with propaganda and provide general assistance. USOM's role was to provide funds and commodities to support the program in general and, more specifically, to help rehabilitate the defectors who had left the Viet Cong. However, no aspect of the Chieu Hoi program received adequate support from the Government of Vietnam, and it has limped along.

It should be emphasized, though the stress in this book is on American activities, that the primary responsibility for pacification or counterinsurgency has remained with the Vietnamese. It was intended that American Provincial Representatives be advisers and teachers, not doers. However, since many of the Vietnamese officials were ill trained and unprepared for provincial jobs, the Americans did more than was originally intended. But the long-term goal has been to help the Vietnamese to run the provinces effectively and responsibly.

The Office of Provincial Operations has been beset with a number of problems, some of which are those that confront any new organization. There was some friction between the new and aggressive Provincial Operations personnel and the regular Agency for International Development employees, who resented its streamlined procedures and disapproved of its grass-roots approach. Furthermore, there was some overlapping of responsibilities, for example, between the Agricultural Division of the United States Operations Mission and Provincial Operations.

Unfortunately, there was frequent change in leadership, which undermined morale and deprived the office of continuity. Phillips left in November, 1963, and his Deputy, Fraleigh, was stricken with hepatitis. Leonard Maynard took charge until February, 1964, when Ogden Williams became the head. The present writer was appointed Associate Director of Provincial Operations in June, 1964, and resigned in December, 1964, at which time his Deputy, Colonel Samuel Wilson, took over. A new Director of the United States Operations Mission, James Killen, was appointed in July, 1964, and made it clear that he did not favor Provincial Operations or some of the people in the office. Though he allowed the work to continue, his attitude hurt morale and efficiency. On the Government of Vietnam side, the coup of November 1, 1963, and the subsequent coups created great instability and led to considerable paralysis in Saigon and the provinces. Province Chiefs and District Chiefs were switched every few months so that, in many cases, the United States Provincial Representative became the one in a province with the longest service and most knowledge about provincial affairs.

During the period 1962–65, the Viet Cong continued to make progress. As their terror and military operations have spread to more and more parts of the country, it has become increasingly difficult for the Vietnamese provincial officials, assisted by the Provincial Representative, to visit these areas—

much less carry out meaningful programs. Without security, social, economic, and political measures cannot be taken except in a very limited and sporadic manner. The military situation appeared, in the fall of 1965, to be improving somewhat, but it is really too early to tell. If it continues to improve and *real* security is provided, this rural program should be expanded and accelerated.

2

VINH BINH PROVINCE

by

W. ROBERT WARNE

Major Le Hoang Thao was Province Chief of Vinh Binh Province. He had been leading inspection groups for a year and a half when he guided a party, including me as the American AID Provincial Representative, to O Dung Hamlet, in the southern part of the province. Thao pointed out the accomplishments of the people in this new strategic hamlet. Beside the long mud wall, groups of farmers were digging traps to complete the rude fortification. Bamboo spikes had already been embedded in the traps along paths that the Viet Cong might use to enter the hamlet. Other farmers were stringing barbed wire along the top of the wall, and women and children were sharpening bamboo spikes to be embedded in the sides of the wall to prevent the Viet Cong from scaling it.

Thao visited the local hamlet council, which met in a newly constructed office finished since his last visit a few weeks earlier. In front of the building, a platoon of young men, formed in ragged lines, drilled awkwardly with American carbines.

Major Thao, dressed in worn army fatigues and a soft

brimmed cap with hanging ear flaps, went out of his way to speak to the elderly people of the hamlet. Several older women smiled in their pleasure at seeing the Province Chief. Thao had a rapport with these people. He paid an allowance, as was a part of his duty on such trips, to the widows of soldiers killed fighting the Viet Cong. He shared coconut milk with the elders as he listened to their problems.

They wanted a new schoolhouse. The present school was a one-room thatched building crammed with seventy students. The people also complained a little. They needed more arms, they said, so the men could effectively defend the hamlet. One platoon was not enough. Major Thao made notes, and then went to the wat to pay his respects to the chief monk. The wat was just beyond the limits of the hamlet.

Major Thao, feeling pressed to meet the national government's requirement that the pacification program be completed by the end of June, 1963, pushed ahead briskly with his inspection tours. Early the next morning, he aroused his party, and we left O Dung. The group walked to Ong Rum Hamlet, three miles from the nearest road. Along the route, a group of farmers misdirected the party so that it took the wrong path and arrived at the hamlet an hour late. This delay was apparently contrived to provide enough time for the local Viet Cong company to set up an ambush. The first warning came when the group was about 200 yards from a line of coconut trees. Several soldiers leading the way drew the first Viet Cong fire. Two of them were killed. The other soldiers, except for one who was seriously wounded, and the remainder of Thao's party dived into a stream bed. The Viet Cong quickly seized the weapons of the wounded and dead soldiers and slunk away. The inspection group remained in the stream bed for half an hour until reinforcements arrived. When Thao and his party finally reached Ong Rum Hamlet, the major wasted no time. He immediately asked the men of the village to cooperate with the government's Strategic Hamlet Program.

The Vietnamese Government started the Strategic Hamlet Program in March, 1962. The strategic hamlets were intended to control the people so that they could not render any assistance to the Viet Cong; the Viet Cong guerrillas would thus be denied access to places in which to rest in security and to receive supplies. By isolating the Viet Cong from the rural people, the government could identify and fix the location of the insurgent troops. This is important in unconventional warfare. In friendly areas, a guerrilla force can fade into the paddy fields, thatched huts, and landscape, hiding their guns and grenades, and take on the appearance of the local farmers.

My visit with Major Thao took place in June, 1963. Vinh Binh had made considerable progress during Thao's term as Province Chief, and he believed that O Dung Hamlet was a successful effort of the embattled country people. Strategic hamlets like O Dung had recently been constructed in many areas of Vinh Binh formerly controlled by the Viet Cong. O Dung, itself, just three months earlier, had been Viet Cong territory.

But it was clear to Major Thao and those of us exposed to Viet Cong tactics that the fifteen-month-old Strategic Hamlet Program was seriously overextended. Yet, the national government persisted in its demands that Vinh Binh Province organize and support more strategic hamlets than it could effectively defend. Thao, who listed 307 hamlets as having armed militia, believed that only about 300 of the 451 strategic hamlets existing in the province in June, 1963, were adequately organized and defended.

Without adequate protection for the local population, the strategic hamlets were vulnerable to Viet Cong counterattack. This meant that unprotected hamlets like Ong Rum were forced to cooperate with the Viet Cong or pay the terrible penalty of Viet Cong terrorism.

There was another drawback to the Strategic Hamlet Program. Ngo Dinh Diem's government misoriented the impact of the program, observers believed, by emphasizing control of the population rather than instituting economic and political activities to win the people's support. Thao was an exception in this regard because of his conscientious effort to win the support of the people. His refusal to force people to relocate into the hamlet perimeter helped to win popular support and stiffened resistance to the Viet Cong, but it reduced the tally of strategic hamlets in the rush pacification programs.

Major Thao left the province shortly after this visit.[1] After the downfall of Ngo Dinh Diem on November 1, 1963, a year of weak provincial administration ensued. Major Thao's loss was felt much more than that of the less experienced and less politically conscious men who followed him in quick succession. The Strategic Hamlet Program itself was terminated by the revolution that overthrew Diem. A new program, the New Life Hamlet Program,[2] was inaugurated in January, 1964. It was clear that the Viet Cong effort in Vinh Binh was now more steadily applied and frequently more intense; there was a sharp increase in Viet Cong forces and in the number of inci-

[1] Major Thao's career illustrates the vagaries of political fortune in South Vietnam. In October, 1965, he was tried by a Vietnamese military court and sentenced to four years in prison for his participation in the abortive *coup d'état* of February 19, 1965.

[2] Since March, 1962, when the Strategic Hamlet Program was initiated by the late President Ngo Dinh Diem, the Government of South Vietnam's rural pacification program has undergone numerous changes. In January, 1964, the Military Revolutionary Council revitalized its rural activities by launching the New Life Hamlet Program, designed to broaden the base of the government's support by gaining the support of the rice farmers through political, economic, and social activities in each hamlet. The New Life Hamlet Program was formally called the Rural Reconstruction Program; but in August, 1965, it was renamed the Rural Construction Program by Prime Minister Nguyen Cao Ky. Prime Minister Ky has made the successful implementation of the New Life Hamlet Program the first priority of his administration. He has placed emphasis on the following: selection and training of cadres to assist the farmers in organizing new life hamlets; decentralization of responsibility and funds for hamlet construction; and the holding of elections and training of local officials to gain popular support for and participation in local government. These various programs are commonly called pacification activities, since their purpose is to secure the countryside and win the support of the rural people.

dents[3] in the post-revolution period as compared with the last years of the Diem regime.

Vinh Binh Province, located in the southwestern region of South Vietnam, is a keystone province in the Mekong Delta area. The province borders two of the principal rivers of the Delta—the Bassac and the Co Chen, which flow into the South China Sea. Vinh Binh is bordered on the northeast by Kien Hoa Province, on the northwest by Vinh Long Province, and on the southwest by Ba Xuyen Province. It is 75 miles south of Saigon by air.

With an area of 1,100 square miles, the province is larger than the average of the 43 provinces that make up Vietnam. The population is 531,000, which is also greater than the provincial average. Throughout the province, the land rises only 1 to 6 yards above sea level, and there are more than 275 miles of streams and canals. Each of the 9 district towns is serviced by a stream or canal, some of them quite sizable. The canal giving access to the provincial capital, Phu Vinh, can accommodate a 250-ton barge. Many of the villages and hamlets also are linked together by streams. Viet Cong activities have now closed some of these waterways to commerce or restricted their use. Consequently, the farmers have been forced to limit shipments of rice and other foodstuffs to Saigon.

The only paved road is the 122-mile national highway connecting Phu Vinh with Saigon. A network of dirt roads connects the towns and hamlets. However, the Viet Cong have destroyed more than 30 important bridges and have dug ditches across many of the roads, thereby greatly disrupting life and commerce.

The Vietnamese farmers live in scattered communities of 500 to 1,500 people situated along waterways and roads. These countryside communities are the hamlets. The average farm

[3] An incident is any Viet Cong-initiated activity against the government or populace, such as a propaganda meeting, kidnaping, assassination, mining, ambush, or attack.

family cultivates between 6 and 12 acres of land and earns the equivalent of $500–$600 a year. For most farmers, the bulk of this income is in rice paddy and other crops.

The farmhouses are built on mud foundations about a yard above the high-water level of the river. The frame of the house, made of wood or saplings, is covered with palm fronds. The house of a poor farmer may have only one or two rooms, with the dining and living quarters frequently used also as sleeping areas. There is a small outside kitchen attached to the house and, frequently, a small addition at the rear to store tools. Here a water buffalo and a pig may be housed, as well. Wood planks supported by sawhorses to serve as beds, a crude wooden table, a few stools, and perhaps one chest of drawers comprise the furniture of the average house.

The diet of the farmer is good. Besides rice, in the Mekong Delta he has fowl and fish. His wife often tends a small vegetable garden beside the house. Fruit trees grow along the stream beds and in scattered groups throughout the hamlet. In prosperous fertile areas, groves of trees are planted as a cash crop. A great variety of fruits are cultivated in Vinh Binh; coconuts, bananas, mangoes, papayas, oranges, tangerines, and grapefruits are the most common. The most important animal in the hamlet is the water buffalo, which is needed for plowing, but there are also cattle, pigs, ducks, and the ever-present, scrawny chickens.

The life cycle of the rice farmer is geared to the tropical weather. The monsoon season begins when the wind shifts and blows from the southwest. At this time, in late April or early May, the farmer prepares his rice-seed beds. Using his buffalo, he plows a small part of the field, carefully rakes the bed, and scatters the rice seed. In forty-five days, he transplants the seedlings into the field.

The farmer is usually dependent on the rains to water his field. During a good year, the paddies are flooded. Frequently, however, the farmer must scoop water from a nearby stream into his paddy to irrigate the rice sufficiently. During a dry year, the Mekong system does not have enough fresh water to flush out the salt water that the tide has carried into the myriad Delta channels from the South China Sea. Without fresh water, the rice land dries out and cracks, and the crop withers. This means hunger and disaster for the countryside.

At harvest time, five to six months after planting, everyone is involved in processing the crop. Some farmers thresh the rice by beating the stalks against the sides of a shed in the field. Others bring the stalks to a threshing circle, where a water buffalo tramples them. The rice is dried in the sun on mats before it is winnowed. For husking and polishing, the rice is taken to a mill, which is frequently owned by a wealthy merchant or landowner. A few farmers in Vinh Binh still have the ancient baskets specially made for husking and polishing. Using two clay-filled baskets, the farmer rapidly rotates the upper basket by swinging a suspended wooden beam attached to the basket. Since this process breaks some of the kernels, and husks the rice unevenly, these mills are not as popular as the larger machine-operated mills. The farmers sell their polished rice to wholesalers, who in turn market it within the province or ship it to Saigon by barge, truck, or bus—the Viet Cong permitting.

Landownership in Vinh Binh is confused since most of the land records were destroyed by the Vietminh. It is estimated that 60 per cent of the farmers do not have title to the land they farm. Only about a third of these now pay rent, because in the insecure areas, the landowners are unable to collect rents. Through the government's Land Reform Service, some tenant farmers are making installment payments to purchase land confiscated from the French and from large Vietnamese landowners. However, the majority of these installment contracts are in arrears at present. In 1958, as a land-reform measure, the government disallowed holdings in excess of 240 acres, but this regulation has not been well enforced. The tenant

George Tanham with Vietnamese village children

The Warne family and village children in Vinh Binh Province

People of a hamlet meet to discuss community needs and to vote on projects

Susanna Warne teaching English in a village high school

Montagnards stream out of the hills of Central Vietnam, fleeing the
Viet Cong

Montagnard refugees in Phu Bon

Buffalo being cooked for *montagnard* ceremony

A well in Vinh Binh Province, built with local labor and U.S. AID-provided materials

farmer is, by law, protected by contracts that the Land Reform Service executed between the landowner and the tenant. These contracts are binding for five years and set rent according to the quality of the land. The maximum rental rate for the best land is 25 per cent of the crop.

Because Vinh Binh is extremely fertile, 80 per cent of its land is cultivated; 90 per cent of this acreage is planted with rice. The second most important crop is fruit, and the third is sugar cane. Sugar cane is an important cash crop in Vinh Binh, where it is grown year round. Some secondary crops are grown principally during the dry season: corn, sweet potatoes, cassava, tobacco, and vegetables. The farmer irrigates these crops by hand from shallow wells. During the dry season, in addition to raising secondary crops, the farmer frequently finds labor in the village or fishes to augment his income.

Life for the average farmer centers around his household, rice field, and hamlet. A trip to the province town, especially for women, may be a once-in-a-lifetime affair. Many farmers own bicycles; those who live near streams may own sampans— lightweight shallow boats of varying sizes. The prosperous farmers have transistor radios.

Several centuries ago, before the Vietnamese settled in Vinh Binh Province, it was sparsely populated by groups who were ethnically Cambodians. During the Vietnamese march southward from the Red River Valley in North Vietnam, the ethnic-Cambodians in large part were driven out. Vinh Binh was settled by the Vietnamese in the first half of the eighteenth century. Many of the Cambodians who remained in the province were driven south to inferior land made salty by tidal waters from the South China Sea, and they eventually lost even that land. Today, a minority group of 130,000 Cambodians live in Vinh Binh. They constitute an important political factor because their strong Buddhist ties unite them against the Viet Cong insurgents. The Cambodians have been slow to assimilate into Vietnamese society. Many of them speak only Khmer, and some have little esteem for the Vietnamese. A Vietnamese official, therefore, must make special efforts to include the Cambodians in the government programs. While this minority may be antagonistic to the Viet Cong, it does not freely give its loyalty to the national government, which it also views as somewhat foreign.

The Cambodians of Vinh Binh are Theravada Buddhists. Their communities are clustered about the 137 wats in Vinh Binh Province. Their religious affiliation determines their way of life, and to reach them, government officials must work through their religious leaders.

The Vietnamese, for the most part, are Mahayana Buddhists. The government states that 65 per cent of the population in Vinh Binh is Mahayana Buddhist, but this group is not nearly so monolithic and loyal to its religious leaders as the Cambodians, and many of the rice farmers do not observe all the religious customs. They maintain ancestral altars in their houses, however, and celebrate the important religious holidays. There are 120 Mahayana temples in the province. In general, however, in Vinh Binh Province, the Mahayana Buddhists do not play as important a role as a group as do the Cambodian Theravada Buddhists.

The Catholic religion was introduced in Vinh Binh Province more than sixty years ago by the French settlers, and today about 9 per cent of Vinh Binh's population is Catholic. This group, too, has political significance, because its priests and laymen are loyal to the national government. Catholic communities are scattered throughout Vinh Binh Province in secure enclaves. Each is clearly marked by a church that usually dominates the community.

The impact of the French settlers was not limited to the religious sphere. The settlers purchased or otherwise acquired much of the best rice land in the province. The French maintained the mandarin hierarchical organization for their colonial administration in Vinh Binh, although French citizens were installed in the posts of Governor of the province and District Chiefs. Vietnamese competed for positions as *fonctionnaires* in the French administration through examinations much like those of the traditional mandarin system, which selected civil servants on the basis of the candidates' knowledge of the Chinese classics. All responsibility and leadership, however, was vested in the French officials. As a result, the French centralized governmental activities under their control in the province capital and the nine district towns. Furthermore, administrative directives and appointments emanated from Saigon. The rural areas continued to be administered through the traditional Confucian-oriented village councils composed of local notables. The seventy-four villages in Vinh Binh were administratively autonomous in many day-to-day operations but were controlled by the central government in matters such as taxes and land titles. The French system paid little attention to the needs and desires of the farmer, but concentrated on having the farmer pay his taxes and rent.

The French constructed a number of roads and bridges in Vinh Binh during their seventy-year rule. In order to improve the water route to Saigon, three important canals were dredged for the transportation of rice. The city of Phu Vinh was provided with a water system, and electrical generators were brought to the most important cities. Most of the district and village markets were constructed during the French period, most of the great houses were built for Frenchmen, and the prominent military installations were manned by French soldiers.

During World War II, the French rule was interrupted by a brief interlude of Japanese occupation. The withdrawal of the Japanese forces left a vacuum in leadership, which the Vietminh prepared to fill. The Vietminh were an amalgamation of the Communists under Ho Chi Minh of the North and Southerners who wanted to establish a Vietnam independent of the French. During the struggle against the French, the Vietminh destroyed many of the landlords' homes and burned the public records of the villages in Vinh Binh. When the French armed the ethnic-Cambodians to help fight the Vietminh, the Vietminh retaliated by burning the warehouses in which the Cambodians stored much of their rice crop. At the same time, the Cambodians killed several thousand Vietnamese in an attempt to gain title to their land. The widespread hunger and distress that resulted, along with these incidents, aggravated the poor relations between the two ethnic groups.

The French suppressed the Vietminh in about three-fourths of the province, but as late as 1954, there remained some areas in which the French did not have effective control. Today many of the burned-out houses still scar the countryside, and the village records have never been reconstructed.

When the French colonial regime ended in 1954, Ngo Dinh Diem succeeded in restoring order and local civil government. Prices became relatively stable, and the farmers were able to market their crops without interference. Vietnamese replaced French administrators without undue interruption in the process of government. In 1959, Diem took measures to entrench his political position throughout the nation. In Vinh Binh, the key political group was the Can Lao (Revolutionary Workers') Party, a small semiclandestine group including several prominent provincial leaders. The Can Lao Party served as the covert leadership corps of the National Revolutionary Movement, which was publicized as the major government party. The wide membership and numerous branches of the National Revolutionary Movement were designed to mobilize public support. However, the Can Lao Party, police agents, and others were directed by Diem's brother Ngo Dinh Nhu to suppress political factions and dissidents. As a result, the populace viewed the National Revolutionary Movement not as a popular political party but as the mechanism through which Nhu selected officials and candidates in order to maintain political control of the province. Similarly, control was maintained over religious groups. A new Buddhist group was formed by the government and sanctioned to direct the religious lives of the Cambodians. In line with Diem's own Catholicism, the Catholic Church continued to be the only religious institution allowed to own rice land, and Catholics often were favored for political offices. Another Diem brother, Bishop Ngo Dinh Thuc, the Apostolic Vicar, provided substantial assistance to local priests in order to maintain the position of the Catholic Church in Vinh Binh.

There can be little doubt that the autocratic and repressive character of Diem's regime, particularly after 1959, helped foster the growth of the Viet Cong, past masters at exploiting popular discontent. The Viet Cong, made up of older Vietminh adherents as well as new recruits, have used the older organization to penetrate Vietnamese society. Just as the Vietminh appealed to the Vietnamese against French imperialism, so the Viet Cong appeal to the spirit of Vietnamese nationalism and use the anti-imperialism theme, directed this time against the United States.

When the war ended in 1954, the genuine nationalists left the Vietminh to join the South Vietnamese Government. In Vinh Binh, for example, many of the present civilian and military officials were enrolled in the Vietminh in the earlier period. By calling themselves a popular front—the National Liberation Front—and capitalizing on the history of the Vietminh as opponents of French colonialism, the Communists today appeal to dissident groups. They have not succeeded, however, in mobilizing popular support in Vinh Binh. Even in the Viet Cong-controlled areas, the Front's leaders are not popular figures, so the leadership remains largely faceless and anonymous.

After the 1954 Geneva Agreements between the French and Vietminh, ending the war and temporarily partitioning the country, the Communists spent nearly five years training cadres in North Vietnam and establishing political cells in vulnerable areas in Vinh Binh. Communist activity increased sharply in mid-1959, when the Viet Cong began military operations to speed up the political takeover. The District Chief of the most southern district in Vinh Binh reported troop landings and squad-size attacks by the Viet Cong in June, 1959. The provincial government ignored these reports until the District Chief was ambushed.

The first ambush established the pattern of Viet Cong military operations. The Viet Cong Provincial Commissar attempted to persuade the people to support the Communist forces. In order to demonstrate his strength, the Provincial Commissar ambushed the District Chief's convoy. The District Chief alone escaped. He sought refuge in a farmer's house, where he hid under a stack of rice straw and eventually escaped. When the Viet Cong learned that he had been given shelter, they returned to the village and assassinated everyone in the farmer's house. This act of terror and revenge successfully discouraged that village from further displays of loyalty to the government. As a result, effective control in that village passed from the provincial government to the Viet Cong.

The development of the Viet Cong forces progressed steadily during the next three years. The first objective was to establish a sanctuary that could be used as an operational base. The National Liberation Front—established in December, 1960, as the political arm of the Viet Cong—gained control by sending a political cadre to each of the rural communities. Wherever they met resistance, armed raiding forces were used to establish control. Hit-and-run tactics were employed against the outposts, bridges, and district offices. The government was forced to relinquish control and draw back its officials, both civilian and military.

By 1963, the southern district was cut off from the rest of the province. Bridges had been blown up and the roads cut off. Interaction of political and military activities on the part of the Viet Cong had either won the support of the local people or intimidated them enough to cooperate. They began paying the costs of supporting the Viet Cong, and no longer supported the government.

The Viet Cong broadened its political and military base throughout the province. Operations were controlled through a Province Committee, which contained specialized sections to implement subversion. The typical Province and District Committees were composed of sections for political espionage, propaganda, operations and training, military intelligence, special espionage, arms production, finance, supply, and administration. The villages and hamlets also had committees similar in organization, which made up a shadow government throughout the province. In areas that the Viet Cong controlled, there was a local budget, information and village offices, and a school. In contested areas, the apparatus was mobile. In government-controlled areas, the Viet Cong were active in intelligence-gathering and propaganda.

The National Liberation Front always directed its military activities to achieve a political goal. To take one example, in mid-1964, one of the Front's targets was the subversion of Catholic communities, in particular, Bai Xon village. Catholic communities are usually the strongest anti-Communist bastions in South Vietnam, and the 10,000 loyal Catholics in Bai Xon had resisted the Front for years. The Viet Cong organized a force of three companies to attack the village. Although the provincial government maintained a military post in the village, the Viet Cong did not attempt to overrun it, but rather sought to contain the government's troops within the post while their political cadres indoctrinated the local populace. At such times, the political cadres discussed seven points with each adult in the village. They spoke of protection of the priests and Church and of freedom of religion. They advocated providing land to each farmer, and promised to prevent the government from drafting men from the village. They said that they would protect the people from the "murderous Khanh," then Premier, and other Vietnamese officials, whom they described as American lackeys. They promised to keep the government from collecting taxes and the landowners from collecting rent. The objective of such attacks was to isolate the government from the people by persuasion and a show of force. Strong efforts were made to neutralize popular figures, such as the priests, by promises of noninterference in religious matters. There was constantly the implied threat of force, which the Viet Cong had already demonstrated. The Viet Cong thus began to separate the loyal people from the government's forces. Once a cell was established within the village, deterioration of morale quickly followed until the village was virtually taken over from within.

In cases where political action is unsuccessful, the Communists have three types of military units to force the village to comply. There is a regular force organized to attack and gain a quick military victory. The regular force slashes at the government's troops and wears down their strength and morale. In Vinh Binh, the Viet Cong increased their regular forces steadily as they enlarged their area of control. From 1963 to 1965, the Viet Cong regular battalions in Vinh Binh Province jumped from one to three.

For small operations, the Viet Cong maintains regional forces which operate in platoon- and company-size units—40 to 120 men in each. At the end of 1964, there were 8 Regional Force companies scattered throughout the province. And, at the base of this pyramid, is the guerrilla, frequently a farmer by day and a soldier by night. These irregular soldiers make up village and hamlet units, which usually range from squad to platoon in size—about 10 to 40 men. There were about 1,200 irregulars in Vinh Binh in November, 1964. The total strength of the Viet Cong at that time in Vinh Binh was about 3,500. There were also several hundred political cadres.

During the early years, 1959 to mid-1963, the Viet Cong relied on its regional and guerrilla forces for most of its military activity. The mission was to take control of remote areas that could be used as operational bases from which to harass government troops. There were no major efforts during this period to take strategic areas of the province. After mid-1963, the Viet Cong greatly accelerated their activities, and more use was made of their regular troops.

July, 1963, marked the beginning of increased military activity. During the first half of 1963, Viet Cong incidents averaged about 25 a month in Vinh Binh province; during the second half of 1964, these incidents increased to about 65 a month, with a high in September of 162 incidents. Through the offensive that was launched immediately after the overthrow of the Ngo Dinh Diem regime, the Viet Cong forced the government to pull in its perimeter defense throughout the province.

In April, 1964, Viet Cong tactics changed. Previously, the local populace had not been intentionally harmed. But now there was a rash of attacks against innocent civilians. The ethnic-Cambodian areas where the people persisted in resisting the Viet Cong were terrorized most severely. Two or three civilian buses were mined each month along roads that the Viet Cong were trying to interdict. Kidnapings and assassinations of civilians, as well as officials, began to occur, and there were even incidents in which whole hamlets were burned. The Viet Cong no longer avoided antagonizing the civil populace.

The Viet Cong had apparently concluded that the combination of political action and implied force had achieved its goal of taking control of the vulnerable areas of the province. Direct force was then resorted to in order to break the resistance of the remaining population. Rural men—often still in their teens—were forcibly recruited into the Viet Cong ranks. Tax rates were sharply increased. Farmers began reporting that they were being compelled to make regular payments in rice to the

Viet Cong, in addition to paying them an annual tax in money of about $10 an acre.

In reaction against the Viet Cong, many elements of the local populace sought support and protection from the Saigon government. The government began to use its artillery and air power to prevent the Viet Cong from concentrating for large attacks. During the closing six months of 1964, this fire superiority was the principal protection for several isolated district towns. The Viet Cong sometimes were able to make political gains, however, during this period as the result of government attacks, often accidental, near a revered pagoda or in a village community. Such attacks angered the people, and the Viet Cong were quick to use them as propaganda against the government. Frequently, the Viet Cong entrenched themselves around a temple deliberately in order to encourage such attacks.

The effectiveness of the versatile soldier who is a propagandist, political cadre, and laborer, as well as a guerrilla, can be demonstrated by the success of the Viet Cong since their buildup in 1959. Roughly 5 per cent of the land area was controlled by the Viet Cong in 1959. In December, 1964, the Viet Cong controlled 25 per cent and operated in another 50 per cent of the province.

Because Viet Cong policy has shifted to include terror against the civilian population, it is possible that the government will have greater success in the future in mobilizing popular support. The Viet Cong, however, are likely to continue to be successful until the government can develop the military means of protecting the rural population and until the civilian officials can eliminate real grievances and thus enable the government to win the support of the people.

The AID Provincial Representative is in charge of the civilian advisory effort in the counterinsurgency program, with a budget of about $100,000 a year in Vinh Binh. He follows up program activities in order to see that they are carried out according to the terms of the agreement. In dealing with the local government, he works primarily as a catalyst to speed its processes. Rather than take an active role in implementing programs himself, he encourages the Vietnamese local officials to take an interest in local problems and to initiate programs to attack these problems. One of the major aims of AID is to build an effective government at the grass roots.

This was a challenging and often frustrating aspect of my job as the Provincial Representative. The Vietnamese *fonctionnaires* who assumed positions of responsibility after the departure of the French officials were ill equipped to administer the province. There was a psychological and cultural gap between the civil servants and the people. The *fonctionnaires*, accustomed to the mandarin and French reliance on centralization of responsibility, initiative, and decision-making, often lacked any concept of political responsiveness to the people. Their position was obtained by examination and education, and promotion was based on seniority rather than performance. Administrative procedures were centralized and specific; the various provincial bureaus and services forwarded matters requiring decision to Saigon in carefully documented dossiers. These factors perpetuated an anonymous civil servant aloof from the local population and with little sense of responsibility or involvement in the war. Therefore, when the AID Provincial Representative sets out to involve the civilian government in the rural areas, he is breaking new ground.

The principal activity of the AID program in the field is supporting the Rural Reconstruction Program, or New Life Hamlet Program, the new name for the Strategic Hamlet Program launched under Diem. Counterinsurgency activities are designed in terms acceptable to the rice farmer. The essential ingredient is the effort to win the support of the people for the government. The process is begun by sending political cadres into rural communities to explain the government's policies. The cadres try to persuade the farmers to support the

construction of a "new-life hamlet"—the successor to the strategic hamlet. A new-life hamlet is oriented toward political
support and popular activities. Concurrent with the political
development in the community, police activities are stepped
up to eliminate the Viet Cong cells and to cut off intelligence
and supplies that support the enemy. An important step in
this development period is the election of a Hamlet Chief and
Hamlet Committee to direct the operations of the community.
Often a vote is not taken, but a consensus is reached among
the venerable leaders—the old men and devout Buddhists in
the community. In order to strengthen the unity of the community, people's groups are organized, among them farmers'
cooperatives, parent-teacher associations, and women's social
groups. The men are encouraged to volunteer for the Popular
Forces that defend the hamlet.

In combination with the political development and organization of the hamlet, military units are brought into the hamlet to protect the people and cadres during the organizational
phase. In priority areas, an Army of Vietnam battalion is stationed at the central village, and a security perimeter is set up
around the adjacent hamlets. In other areas, the district Regional Force company is used with the village Popular Force
unit in providing local security. These troops are expected to
remain in the area until the residents and local militia are
able to protect themselves, but when emergencies develop in
other areas, security forces are often pulled out before local
security units have been trained and are in place. In such
cases, the Viet Cong are able to disrupt the work of the cadres
by re-entering the hamlet to propagandize the people and to
threaten those who have cooperated with the government.
Adequate security is clearly a prerequisite to the implementation of the New Life Hamlet Program.

Countrymen are encouraged to volunteer for the Popular
Forces, which the government organizes and pays as the local
defense force in the hamlet. There are advantages for the ham-

let residents in joining the Popular Forces. Most important to a farmer is that he can continue to live with his family and to farm his land. A salary equal to the wages of an agricultural laborer (about $13.50 a month), uniforms, and a weapon are provided. The recruits for the hamlet defense force are volunteers who receive six weeks of training in the provincial training center. Squad and guerrilla tactics are taught along with markmanship. The unit leader is an experienced soldier, such as a former sergeant with the Vietminh or French forces. Arms for the Popular Forces come from the American Military Assistance Program. They include carbines, riot shotguns, and hand grenades. This program of integrating the local defense force into the Popular Forces is a great improvement over the poorly organized and ill-equipped defense forces of Diem's Strategic Hamlet Program.

In Vinh Binh, most completed new-life hamlets have a Popular Force unit ranging from squad to platoon size—10 to 40 men. Many of the hamlets have fortified the council hall to be used as the unit's headquarters or have built a separate post. A walkie-talkie radio or telephone is set up in the hamlet so that the village can be reached quickly in case of emergency. The nearest village usually has a platoon of soldiers that can reinforce the hamlet. Ammunition and arms are stored in the headquarters, but the hamlet soldiers usually live in their own houses.

It was my experience that these self-defense units were effective in Vinh Binh when the local District Chief supervised and supported each hamlet. In the ethnic-Cambodian areas, where morale was high and the men had previous fighting experience, the hamlet defense system was outstanding. There were frequent instances of small units fighting off large Viet Cong forces without losing any weapons. The defense system was also effective in Catholic communities. There were also incidents of inexperienced units being easily overrun or of the Viet Cong planting a traitor within the unit who enabled

them to enter the hamlet or ambush the unit. Soldiers sometimes ran out of ammunition and funds owing to the failure
of the District Chief to visit the hamlet regularly.

Small units were not expected to fight when outnumbered.
The preferable tactic was for the hamlet soldiers to withdraw to the village or, if there was no escape route, to use a
fortified position until reinforcements arrived. The Popular
Forces were, as a result, dependent upon prompt reinforce-
ment. Morale consequently corresponded to the reliability of
the village and district to respond quickly and drive off large
Viet Cong attacks. In some districts, the Regional Forces
were ineffective, particularly at night, which undercut morale
among the Popular Forces and made the results of the New
Life Hamlet Program marginal at best.

Besides political development and military security, the
government provided economic and social projects that demonstrated the government's role in helping the people of the
hamlet. These were known as self-help activities because projects were built by voluntary labor. The procedure was this:
The cadre called a meeting to discuss an improvement project.
The most popular projects were a school, a first-aid station, a
market, a bridge, a cement-lined well, a community pigsty,
and an irrigation canal. The province government provided
materials, such as cement and aluminum roofing, and funds to
purchase sand, stone, and wood and to pay for skilled labor.
The people, in turn, agreed to construct the project. Community development served to unify the hamlet and to enhance
the government's prestige. There was less opportunity for corruption in self-help because the community was involved in
supervising the purchasing and the use of materials. Also, the
Viet Cong were not so likely to destroy a self-help project as a
contract project. The community that had built a self-help
project valued it and whoever might destroy it would win
their hatred.

In Vinh Binh, the self-help project idea took nearly a year

to implement. The government at first lacked trust in the people's ability to construct their own projects, and the people of the hamlet were not accustomed to working together on community improvement. Once the idea took hold, the AID Mission had difficulty supplying sufficient cement, roofing, and funds to keep up with requests. During the two-year period of 1963 and 1964, more than 500 projects were undertaken and more than 300 communities enjoyed the benefits of self-help. Sometimes the impact of these projects was reduced by petty corruption or inept administration, but for the most part, this was the most successful activity in the Rural Reconstruction Program.

The government also helped the farmer through numerous activities that were managed by the local officials of the national ministries. The Ministry of Agriculture made the greatest impact in Vinh Binh through its rice-improvement and credit activities. During 1964, the goal was to increase rice production by 25 per cent in the secure areas. An improved variety of rice seed, developed in Taiwan, was distributed. This seed, if used properly, increased production by 20 per cent. More than 2,000 tons of fertilizer were sold to hamlet farmers on credit. Credit was also provided to purchase pigs, chickens, and water buffaloes. The Ministry of Health had a program to train, pay, and supply medicine to a resident who set up a first-aid station in a hamlet. The Ministry of Education trained and paid schoolteachers to serve the hamlet schools, which included the self-help schools. Textbooks and school supplies were also provided. In larger communities, the Ministry of Public Works undertook rural electrification by selling generators on credit and setting up a utility plant. Recently these ministerial programs, except the health program, were integrated into the AID Provincial Rehabilitation Agreements so that the Provincial Coordinating Committee has supervisory responsibility over these program areas.

During the first year and a half of the hamlet program,

March, 1962, to November, 1963, when it was called the Strategic Hamlet Program, families were forcibly moved into the fortified perimeter of the hamlet. The purpose was to consolidate the hamlet by relocating outlying families—roughly 20 per cent of the households. In some cases, whole hamlets were composed of transplanted residents. In Vinh Binh, force was used infrequently, but cajoling and payments of money were applied to encourage the remote households to join the strategic hamlet. After the overthrow of the Diem administration, the policy was changed so that only volunteers were relocated into the new-life hamlets. Funds were provided in the AID agreement to pay costs of moving into the community, but the number of families that moved dropped sharply. In 1963, more than 3,000 families relocated, but under the voluntary program in 1964, only about 700 moved. The government belatedly recognized that the people's support could not be won by disrupting their life and moving their households away from their rice fields and their ancestral graves.

During 1964, the success of the New Life Hamlet Program was only marginal in seven of the nine districts in Vinh Binh. Despite the impact of constructive projects for the rural farmer, security in Vinh Binh deteriorated, and the hamlet program amounted to a holding operation rather than expanding controlled areas. This does not necessarily invalidate the concept of the hamlet program. Its shortcomings lie in implementation and attitude, not in theory. In fact, in their "liberated" areas, the Viet Cong are constructing "combat hamlets," which are similar to the government's own.

The majority of the rice farmers have no ideological loyalty toward either the government or the Viet Cong. The farmer's loyalties are to his family and farm; he wants to be left alone and to enjoy peace. Conversations with farmers disclose an order of priority in rural needs. First is security and protection, which can be offered only by the side that has military superiority in the farmer's area. The New Life Hamlet Program is designed to protect the farmer through a local defense force and adequate village and district forces to prevent successful large Viet Cong attacks. Effective protection, however, requires more than just numbers of soldiers, because the Viet Cong try to subvert the hamlet from within by setting up intelligence cells, exploiting weaknesses of the government, and psychologically controlling the people.

The organization of Tan An Luong village in Vinh Binh illustrates the complexities of the problem. A battalion of government troops provided protection while political cadres organized the people and conducted investigations to uncover the Viet Cong cells. After the battalion was removed, security in Tan An Luong rapidly deteriorated. Viet Cong cadres returned to propagandize the people and collect taxes. The Popular Force platoon was attacked and driven into the local fortified post. Consequently, the village became insecure at night. The school and bridge, which had been built as self-help projects, were partly destroyed by Viet Cong mines. The people never gained confidence in the new-life hamlet, because they continued to be intimidated by Viet Cong agents secretly in their midst, and they knew that government forces would never stay long enough to establish real security.

The second desire of the rural Vietnamese is for a fair, adequate local government. This need exists particularly at the village level, where the village council provides documents such as birth and marriage certificates, identification cards, permits for travel out of the village areas, and registration of land titles. Tax collection and preparation and enforcement of draft lists are also the responsibility of the village council. In fact, there are cases where a village chief has imprisoned a farmer or expropriated his land illegally. Although there are statutes and a provincial court to protect the rights of a citizen, litigation is cumbersome and expensive, and the village chief's position far outweighs that of a farmer.

The farmer is aware of the importance of a village chief who has "humanity." To the farmer, this means that the village office acts promptly and treats him with respect and fairness. Despite material assistance from Saigon, poor local administration can undo the government's efforts. For example, in Hiep Hoa village, a new market, school, and dispensary were constructed, but the people had an apathetic spirit. The Province Chief investigated. An old woman said that her land had been taken for the site of the clinic. Another resident complained that only half the cement that was sent to the village was used for the market. As a result, the foundation was unsound. The schoolteacher failed to open the school. In this village, the Province Chief's quick investigation made it possible to correct these abuses.

The third need of the farmer is assistance in improving his lot. Many remote areas have none of the community facilities a government is expected to provide. They had neither a sanitary well nor a schoolhouse. The farmer must take his wife five or more miles for maternity care. When a disaster strikes, a fire, a flood, or a drought, the community is destitute. Effective government makes a great impact upon the farmer in such a place by assisting in improving the community. The provincial government, through the AID Provincial Rehabilitation Agreement, has the ability to do just that. Besides the many self-help projects, funds and food are available to help in disasters. Contingency funds were used, for example, to make loans to Tra Cu District when a drought withered the riceseed beds and the farmers had no money to purchase additional seed. After a fire destroyed 100 houses in Cau Ngang District town, the province provided roofing and cement to rebuild the houses.

Experience indicates that the New Life Hamlet Program meets the basic needs of the people for protection, fair government, and development. Nevertheless, several shortcomings have seriously impeded the program, and security in Vinh Binh was deteriorating in 1964. Although the principles were sound, implementation of hamlet construction left a lot to be desired.

A principal drawback was the turnover of Province Chiefs and consequent slowdowns and changes of direction.[4] Another problem was inadequate direction and supervision from the central government owing to its lack of stability. The province often had no guidance in program implementation during late 1963 and 1964, which paralyzed activity on the part of cautious public servants. Even when directives were forthcoming, officials lacked motivation and neglected the critical remote areas out of fear. On the hamlet level, the political cadres did not have sufficient commitment and dedication to win the people's support. The real problems in Vinh Binh, as a result, were not so much monetary or material but human—the shortage of qualified, dedicated people to organize productive activities. Of course, there are highly dedicated Vietnamese civil servants who risk their lives to help the people, but there are too few of them.

The American advisory effort worked to correct these human shortcomings.[5] Setting the example of working hard and traveling widely, the AID Representative encouraged similar responses from the Vietnamese. Support in decision-making developed confidence and decisiveness on the part of inexperienced officials. The American adviser found that an approach of friendship and respect was important; the warm responses

[4] After the departure of Major Thao in July, 1963, three Province Chiefs followed in quick succession in Vinh Binh. Finally, in July, 1964, an experienced regimental commander, Lieutenant Colonel Nguyen Van Thanh, took office. As of October, 1965, Colonel Thanh remained in office as Vinh Binh Province Chief. Reports in 1965 indicate that the hamlet program is slowly restoring security in those areas held by the Viet Cong.

During my tour in Vinh Binh, I also worked with four energetic and dedicated senior military advisers: Major William A. Rawn, Major Leland C. Flynn, Major James H. Sellers, and Major Joseph E. Muckerman.

[5] American civilian advisers in Vinh Binh came from all levels of the AID Mission. During my tour in Vinh Binh, my supervisors, particularly Ralph A. Harwood, Jr., and George H. Melvin, aided me greatly and assisted in advising the provincial officials. There were also technicians from the AID Mission who contributed to the advisory effort in the province. The following technicians worked in Vinh Binh most frequently: Dr. Charles D. Crocker, agriculture adviser; Dr. Daniel J. Hays, education adviser; Blake Wallace, public-safety adviser; and Robert B. Clary, public-administration adviser.

it produced improved the reception of his advice. Patience and an appreciation for the problems of the provincial official, particularly the political pressures he faced, helped to develop an effective relationship. The adviser, civilian or military, had to take pains not to make the local official's decision for him, and the Vietnamese had to retain responsibility for the conduct of the war.[6] Since the Viet Cong charged that Americans were imperialists, the adviser had to take care to avoid lending credence to this propaganda.

Several families of field AID employees lived in the provincial capitals before the withdrawal of dependents in February, 1965. The families often contributed to the local community, which demonstrated the intentions of the Americans to work on equal terms with the Vietnamese. My wife taught at the high school in Phu Vinh during the day. In the evening, she organized English classes for adults and young people, attended by 200 Vietnamese. The officers of the U.S. Military Advisory Command assisted in the classes.[7] All these activities constituted part of the job of working shoulder to shoulder with the Vietnamese to promote improved security and a better life in the rural areas.[8]

[6] The provincial advisory team in Vinh Binh relied on the assistance of other Free World countries and Vietnamese. Despite narrow escapes from a Viet Cong mine and ambush during his first week in Vinh Binh, Manuel de Vera, a Philippine national, persisted in making regular trips to assist in self-help construction. Trang Tru, my Vietnamese assistant, lived and worked with me for more than eighteen months despite the fact that he was under fire from the Viet Cong more than thirty times.

[7] Among them were Captain A. E. Brown, Jr., and Captain R. E. Faulkender, Civil Guard and Popular Force advisers; Captain F. S. Nuffer, Jr., civil affairs adviser; and Captain W. F. LaCombe, intelligence adviser.

[8] Arnold J. Radi, previously with the International Voluntary Service in Laos, replaced me in December, 1964, as Provincial Representative in Vinh Binh. His bride of three months lived in Phu Vinh until dependents were evacuated in February, 1965. Arny Radi nevertheless continued on in Vinh Binh as the AID Provincial Representative until June, 1965. Ismael Zapatar replaced Radi, and after only a month on the job, his AID jeep was hit by a Viet Cong mine while he was driving on the national highway in Vinh Binh. Fortunately, neither Zapatar nor David A. Engle, an officer from the American Embassy who was also in the jeep, was seriously hurt.

3

PHU BON PROVINCE

by
EARL J. YOUNG

OUR JEEP CLIMBED out of the valley, topped the first rise, and the city of Pleiku vanished abruptly from sight behind us. I felt like an ocean castaway whose ship had just disappeared beneath the sea. In front of the Jeep, Highway 14 stretched out across the empty face of the High Plateau, a winding black ribbon making a lonely trek through the land of the *montagnards*. Even though I had rested in Pleiku for only a few hours, I still had a very clear impression of the sprawling air base and its swarm of busy helicopters, of the streets crowded with American and Vietnamese soldiers, of the friendly little side-street bars with blaring music and pretty young hostesses. This was November 20, 1962, and I was on the final leg of a journey to Phu Bon Province, my first assignment with the Agency for International Development in Vietnam.

Phu Bon is a new province, created in September, 1962, from three desolate districts of Pleiku, Darlac, and Binh Dinh Provinces. This area is much like that of our own newly created Territories in the early days of the West. Only a handful of fearful and unhappy Vietnamese lowland farmers live along the highways and river valleys. The rest of the new province is a hunting ground for tigers, elephants, warring mountain tribes, and the Viet Cong. Phu Bon lies in the foothills of the mountain chain that extends north from Saigon through the heart of Vietnam to China. This land has been the traditional home of the *montagnards*, seminomadic non-Vietnamese hill tribes, for centuries. A sturdy and independent race, these *montagnards* were the original inhabitants of this area, and have engaged in intermittent conflict with the Vietnamese for hundreds of years. Their total number in Vietnam, perhaps 800,000, and their strategic location along the Laotian border—and deep into North Vietnam—have given them a great significance in the war between the Viet Cong and the government. For this reason, several American AID Provincial Representatives were assigned, in the fall of 1962, to provinces with large *montagnard* populations.

The first part of my trip—225 miles from the Saigon Airport to the military air base at Pleiku—had taken less than two hours. The final leg, from Pleiku to Cheo Reo, capital of Phu Bon Province, took four hours by Jeep. This 58-mile stretch of uneven, rock-strewn road is occasionally interdicted by a Viet Cong ambush, but more often marked only by the tracks of wandering tigers.

In the lead Jeep, I could see Major Pham Dinh Chi, the Vietnamese Province Chief, in earnest conversation with our American Military Sector Adviser, Major Clement Will, who had been in the province for the past two months.

Major Chi, a reserve officer in the Vietnamese Army, had been recalled to active duty and served initially at II Corps Headquarters in Pleiku until being assigned as the first Province Chief of Phu Bon. Before leaving his family in Pleiku, Major Chi had invited Major Will and me to his home there. Ba (Mrs. Chi) was a very attractive woman, slim and graceful in her traditional Vietnamese *ao-dai*, with the high-standing collar and close-fitting long-sleeved bodice that gives the gown a very formal look. The Chis' four chidren were shy and hesitant at first, but I had a bag of American chocolate candy, which made an instant hit, and the youngsters soon clustered around. Major Chi, like all Vietnamese fathers, was very proud of his family and pleased that I had brought something for the children. I felt that a good start had been made. Strategy talks in Saigon had made it evident that our personal relations with the Province Chief would be a key factor in the radically new attempt to build up the responsiveness of the local government to its citizens, Vietnamese and *montagnards* alike.

In common with the practice of most governments in Southeast Asia, officials in Vietnam are generally appointed, not elected. This method, stemming from the mandarin tradition, may have produced intellectual leaders in the past, but it certainly focused the attention of the official upward to the government that had appointed him, not downward to the people whom he had to rule. Centuries of government under this system have all but eliminated official responsiveness to the needs of the population. Equal opportunity and social justice are new terms in Southeast Asia, where democratic elections as we know them are held only in Japan, the Philippines, and Malaysia.

Through personal friendship with President Diem, some Americans were able to persuade him to undertake the experiment of decentralizing the Saigon government's authority in favor of the provinces. This was the first step in the attempt to persuade the Vietnamese that local government should be the servant, not the master, of its citizens. While Saigon approved in principle, it still remained for each newly assigned American Provincial Representative to persuade and assist the Vietnamese Province Chief to put this new idea into practice. This was the beginning of a great effort that continues to this day; to convince the Vietnamese that they must fight the Communist-led Viet Cong not only with guns but also with the most

effective weapon of all—a responsive government truly interested in the welfare of its people.

Major Chi, with whom I was to work during the next ten
months, was, like most Vietnamese, an exceedingly complex
person. He was short and slight of build by American standards, looking much younger than his forty-two years. He spoke
excellent French and good English. His attention to protocol
and precedence were worthy of a vice consul. Thus far, his
reaction to my presence had been cordial and correct, but it
was not difficult to detect his underlying reserve. In this respect, he was matched by his American military counterpart.
I could see that both Major Chi and Major Will were a little
dubious about the addition of an American civilian to the ex-
clusively military configuration of the province. Because of the
long insurgency and the shortage of trained civilian officials,
the leadership structure throughout the country is almost entirely military. Province Chiefs, District Chiefs, and most of
their staffs are military personnel. By training and experience,
their approach and solutions to problems facing the province
are military ones. It remained to be seen if I could fit in and
make a contribution under these circumstances. I hoped that
my previous experience as an army officer might help to bridge
the gap.

Major Will, a tall, well-built Texan, was an artillery officer
by profession. He had been assigned to give military assistance
to the new province. We were to be the American "one-two"
punch, Major Will providing military expertise and I recom-
mending improvements on the civilian side of the government.

As we journeyed toward Cheo Reo, we came upon a group
of *montagnards* by the side of the road. They were in single
file, in the custom of mountain people who have spent their
lives on narrow paths in the deep forest or over mountain
passes. My curiosity was obvious to the driver, who braked the
Jeep to a crawl and, nodding at the group, said: "Jarai." This is
the name given to members of the second largest *montagnard*

tribal group in Vietnam. The Jarai regarded us with equal curiosity. But when I waved, they broke into wide grins, disclosing front teeth filed down to the gum. This American habit of smiling and waving at groups we passed never failed to amaze the Vietnamese. They found it especially hard to understand why we bothered to acknowledge the existence of the *montagnards*, who always responded with great friendliness. The Jarai in Phu Bon usually acknowledged my wave by making a stiff, jerky bow, holding their arms clasped across their chests. The children in particular responded with this bow, a gesture of respect taught them at school. It always embarrassed me, and American visitors from Saigon who witnessed this practice never failed to make pointed remarks about the "colonialists" in Phu Bon. During my three years in the Far East, I found the mountain tribes quite receptive to a friendly smile and any gesture of friendship. This often led to an invitation to visit their homes. In the mountains of northwest Thailand, Laos, and Vietnam, the axiom that a smile is an international password is borne out by my experience.

I looked at these Jarai with interest, for this was my first real contact with the mountain people. Their skins were dark and leathery, in contrast to the urban Vietnamese, who took great pride in their fair skins. These Jarai were short but sturdy, walking the highway with an air of dignity and independence. Despite the heavy loads of wood they carried in woven baskets on their backs, they had an upright carriage. The women wore a rough wraparound cotton skirt, and most had no upper garment. Their bodies were firm and muscular from work and constant exposure to the tropical sun. Their breasts were high and full, and their black, oily hair was pulled back into a bun at the nape of the neck. Several women were smoking the local version of a cigar, a kind of loosely rolled green leaf.

The men in general seemed to be wearing only a loincloth, a long, narrow strip of black cloth wrapped around the waist, passed between the legs from the rear and then pulled through the waistband in front. They were, like the women, barefoot. Despite the scantiness of their garb, however, the *montagnards* are very modest. When they take their evening bath in a nearby stream, they walk into the water with their skirt or loincloth in place, and pull it up slowly as the water level rises.

Some of the men we passed on the road carried infants on their backs, the youngsters held in place with wide bands of cloth passed around both father and child. This custom is common among most mountain tribes in Vietnam, where the father often carries the children, especially the male offspring. This is not an assumption of the woman's role; it means rather that the father takes great pride in his children and wants to be with them. In many mountain tribes, a man's wealth and status in the village are measured by the number of his sons.

Many of the men we passed had a knife thrust through the band of their loincloth and carried short, powerful-looking crossbows. I learned that these crossbows—firing poisoned-tipped arrows that are usually kept in a hollow section of bamboo hanging at the waist—could bring down deer and even tigers, both of which are plentiful in the area.

As we passed the end of the column, the impact of the long and bloody Viet Cong war was evident. The last four young *montagnards* were riding bicycles and had American Thompson submachine guns slung across their backs. In addition to the usual loincloth, they wore faded army shirts several sizes too large, and a web cartridge belt holding ammunition and several hand grenades. These young men were part of the local hamlet Self-Defense Force, trained and armed by the U.S. Special Forces to protect their homes against the Viet Cong. They were accompanying the little group to the marketplace, for the Viet Cong often took this opportunity to collect taxes or kidnap young men for their guerrilla force.

At Plei Khe, twenty miles south of Pleiku, there is a fork in the road. To the right, Highway 14 continues on to Ban Me Thuot, in Darlac Province. To the left, Highway 7 plunges off

the High Plateau and follows the river valley through Phu Bon
Province and on to the city of Tuy Hoa, on the sandy shore of
the South China Sea. Our security force had waited here at the
road junction for our return, since no trouble had been antici-
pated between this point and Pleiku. Our Jeep stopped, and I
walked with Major Chi and Major Will as they checked the
convoy. Leading off was a 1939-vintage French armored car.
From inside the steel-sided monster came the angry squawk-
ing of several ducks, which the crew had purchased during our
absence. Next in line was an American World War II truck,
carrying two squads of the Phu Bon Civil Guards, armed to
the teeth with submachine guns, hand grenades, and carbines.
Then came our Jeeps, followed by another truckload of soldiers. Finally, bringing up the rear, an ambulance. I regarded
this last vehicle with mixed feelings. Its usefulness was beyond
question, but its implications were pessimistic, even ominous.

There was a confused shouting of orders, men napping under nearby trees got back in the trucks, weapons were checked,
helmets were adjusted, and we were off for Cheo Reo in a
cloud of dust. Within a few miles, the road began to drop
down from the plateau into the Ia Ayun River Valley. The
red clay soil of the Highlands was replaced now with rich
black loam. The lush vegetation of the rain forest overhung
the edges of the road, but we had no time to appreciate the
beauty of the place. One thought was in everyone's mind: this
was an excellent spot for a Viet Cong ambush! The convoy
seemed determined to destroy itself without any help from the
Viet Cong, as it careened around the turns and roared at full
speed along any relatively straight stretch of road.

The Vietnamese application of Oriental fatalism is nowhere
better typified than in their method of preparing for an enemy
ambush. Any other army in the world would send scouts
ahead, looking for signs of the enemy or trying to trigger the
ambush prematurely with a small force. Scouts would also be
posted to the rear and whenever possible to the flanks to pro-

vide all-around protection. But the Vietnamese concept is simply to put everyone in the middle of the road and go like hell! This procedure at best gives the American military adviser gray hair. At worst, it is responsible for a large number of unnecessary casualties and destroyed vehicles.

It was beginning to grow dark, and the already appreciable tension went up several notches. My own stomach muscles tightened and the whole character of the highway became more menacing. In the midst of the forest, we suddenly came upon a sign suspended above the road. In faded orange letters, I read the words: TINH PHU BON. We had just crossed the boundary into Phu Bon Province. Now if we were attacked, it would be by the local provincial Communist guerrilla force. This did not really seem to improve the situation.

In a matter of minutes, the convoy was skidding down the sharp, hairpin descent of Chu Dre Pass, and the whole panorama of the valley of the Song Ba stretched out ahead. The setting sun cast long shadows across the valley, and I could almost hear a collective sigh of relief as we made the final turn and left the pass with its mountains and jungle behind. The Vietnamese seemed to feel at home once more, driving through the rice fields they knew so well. We still had an hour's drive ahead, but it was through the fertile river valley, dotted with newly constructed strategic hamlets and patrolled by government forces.

Cooking fires were burning in the *montagnard* hamlets as we passed, and little children ran to the road to watch our convoy. Later we rattled across a small wooden bridge and drove down the wide, dusty main street of Cheo Reo. The journey was over.

One night several months later, the roar of artillery fire wakened me. Shoving aside the heavy woolen blanket, I looked at my watch. It was just past midnight, the beginning of another day in the Republic of Vietnam.

The cool night air carried the sound of the Vietnamese gun crews reloading the 105 howitzers. The guns were dug in only a few yards from the American compound. Inside this barbed-wire enclosure were the three olive-drab tents that housed the U.S. advisory effort in Phu Bon Province: eight military men and myself, the lone civilian. We had grown accustomed to regular firing by the artillery, but this midnight cannonade indicated that someone had pushed the panic button and pushed it hard!

Throwing on some clothes, I left the tent and climbed aboard the Jeep taking Major Will to Provincial Headquarters. The focal point in any crisis, the Provincial Headquarters building served as both the seat of government and as a military command post for the Vietnamese. As we pulled up near headquarters, our headlights picked out a company of sleepy Civil Guard soldiers, strapping on their packs as they hurriedly formed up beside the stucco building.

Inside, Major Chi was engaged in an animated conversation with Captain Tang, his military deputy, and Captain Phuoc, Commander of the Phu Bon Civil Guard Battalion. They were standing before a large wall map, studying the nearby district of Phu Thien. I listened closely as they explained to Major Will that an outpost on the opposite bank of the Song Ba had heard heavy firing in the vicinity of one of the *montagnard* strategic hamlets. I knew that men in the hamlet had been trained and armed, but they were not expected to defend themselves against a superior Viet Cong force for an extended time. This was apparently the first enemy action against one of our strategic hamlets, and I was very concerned about the outcome. Major Chi had given orders for the artillery to open fire near the hamlet in an effort to discourage the enemy from launching an assault. This explained the night-time bombardment.

Major Will and the three Vietnamese officers were soon deep in the details of military tactics. The room was filled with the high-pitched crackle of the field radio, a direct link with the outpost across the river. Every soldier in the room was busily engaged in some vital task; they all had a job to do except me.

Major Chi and Major Will took for granted my concern over the conduct of the impending battle. Yet I felt useless in the face of this direct confrontation with the enemy. As the USOM representative, I had helped to provide technical advice, tools, and medicines for the Strategic Hamlet Program, but the outcome of this battle would be determined in the end by the guns and guts of the shy and uncomplaining *montagnards* in the hamlet. What use was our economic aid at a time like this? It would not stop bullets. Perhaps Chairman Mao Tse-tung was right; all power did flow from the barrel of a gun.

The advisability of sending an immediate relief force to the hamlet was under discussion as another radio message came from the outpost. All sounds of firing had ceased in the vicinity of the hamlet. The soldiers waiting outside in the darkness were spared a midnight march through the jungle; it was decided to wait until first light before dispatching troops.

I left the military pondering the situation and walked back through the cool night air to my tent. It was just past one o'clock in the morning. I had a feeling it was going to be a long day in Phu Bon.

At breakfast, some hours later, only Major Will and one of his sergeants were in the mess tent. The other officers had left at daybreak for the threatened hamlet. As personal military adviser to the Province Chief, Major Will accompanied Major Chi at all times; if the Province Chief conducted a military operation, Major Will went with him. If Major Chi elected to remain at his headquarters, so did Major Will. This time I think Major Will was not unhappy that the Province Chief had decided to remain in Cheo Reo. In order to reach the hamlet, the Song Ba had to be forded on foot, and I had seen several hungry crocodiles taken from the river. During breakfast, our thoughts were on the relief column making its way through the forest. But until a further report came in, we must carry on our routine daily business.

The formal schedule for the day was pretty full; at ten o'clock a meeting of the Provincial Committee was to be held; this included Major Chi, Major Will, and me. The purpose of the meeting was to discuss the growing refugee problem and the status of the various USOM-financed projects. Immediately after that session, I planned to visit a local French missionary priest who had been collecting weather data for many years. Since the new province did not yet have an agricultural service, we hoped to gain some local information on the amount and duration of the rainfall. This would help in selecting new varieties of crops that could be grown by the *montagnards*. There were only a few other Westerners in Phu Bon—two French priests and an American Protestant missionary and his family. At twelve-thirty, a chartered USOM plane was due to arrive carrying Dr. Emmanuel (Manny) Voulgaropoulos and Joe Haritani. They were two top-notch American medical specialists with the USOM Public Health program in Vietnam. At our urgent request, they were coming to look over the health aspects of the refugee problem, which involved 11,000 mountain people who had left the jungle-covered mountainsides and streamed into the government-controlled river valley. To bring the official day to a smashing close, the *montagnard* tribal chieftains planned a ceremony with the sacrifice of five buffaloes. This was my first full-dress Jarai ceremony, and I was looking forward to it with great interest. Fortunately, I didn't know what was to be required of the participants. From experience, I knew that fifty problems of minor or major importance would pop up during the course of the day, but we tried at least to start each day in a planned, efficient manner.

Our breakfast came to an end as an ancient Jeep, a battered

relic of World War II, swung off the dirt road and braked to a squeaky stop beside the mess tent. Major Will's only expression of professional disapproval was a slight grimace as he noted the disreputable appearance of the vehicle and its occupants. Two men piled out of the Jeep and walked over to the tent. Their work-stained fatigues and worn, unshined jungle boots contrasted sharply with the starched, highly polished appearance of our regular military advisers. It wasn't necessary to see the low-slung pistols and jaunty green berets to identify the newcomers as two members of the U.S. Army's Special Forces Team—Captain Stogner and Sergeant Garafolo.

Entering the tent, both made a determined effort at military protocol by directing a hearty chorus of "Good morning, sir" at Major Will. At the same time, they looked hopefully at the steaming pot of coffee on the table. Major Will caught the glance and invited them to join us. Sergeant Garafolo volunteered the information that they were out of coffee and had not been able to buy any on the local market, but Headquarters had promised to send coffee with the next air drop of supplies, scheduled for this morning.

Captain Stogner and his eleven-man team had been in Phu Bon only a few weeks. They were the first Special Forces Team to be assigned to the province and faced a tough job. Their assignment was similar to that of the other Special Forces units in the country: to recruit, train, and lead local citizens in operations against the Viet Cong guerrillas. Here in the Central Highlands, the soldiers would usually be *montagnard* tribesmen. This program was an effort to help the Vietnamese Army by establishing an antiguerrilla force to meet the enemy on his home ground. The Special Forces paid well, and provided their CIDG (Civil Irregular Defense Group) with good weapons, good uniforms, medical care, and, above all, friendship. The close bond between the *montagnards* and the Special Forces Teams has been viewed with suspicion by the Vietnamese, and on several occasions, skilled *montagnard* political leaders tried to further their own ambitions by playing off the Americans against the Vietnamese.

The twelve Americans who make up a Special Forces "A" Team are unusual individuals. Each man must be highly proficient in a special skill to win a place on the team. Some are experts in small arms, others in radio communications, explosives, or medical technology. Captain Stogner, a tough, wiry man from the Ozark country, was a true natural to be commander of the first team in the province. Sergeant Garafolo was the Operations specialist.

Until the introduction of American combat units in mid-1965, the Special Forces Teams were the only U.S. soldiers fighting as units in South Vietnam. Their morale was high, despite the isolated and dangerous nature of their mission.

There was usually a close working relationship between the Special Forces and the local USOM representative. The combination of skills, funds, and materials possessed by both were of great assistance to the rural-development program. The Special Forces Team in Phu Bon assisted in the strategic-hamlet rural-development program in a number of ways. They temporarily undertook the task and training and arming *montagnards* who were willing to participate in the defense of their hamlets. The *montagnards* were quite pleased to receive the small but deadly 30-caliber carbines issued by the team. In addition to purposes of self-defense, these made excellent hunting weapons, far surpassing the crossbow. I have seen a number of large tigers shot and killed with the carbine, which is no mean accomplishment. The Special Forces medical personnel also agreed to train hamlet health workers for each of our planned 147 new hamlets. USOM, through the local Vietnamese Government, provided a training allowance and a new medicine chest with a supply of 13 basic drugs for trainees who finished the 30-day course conducted by the Special Forces.

USOM also provided a salary of 600 piasters per month to all graduates of the Special Forces health course who returned to work in their hamlets.

This cooperation among the Vietnamese Government, the U.S. Army Special Forces Team, and the U.S. Operations Mission (AID) certainly paid off in Phu Bon. As we sat around the table, our conversation turned almost immediately to the problem of implementing the Strategic Hamlet Program in Phu Bon. Captain Stogner, Major Will, and I compared notes on what we had learned so far.

The attitude of the *montagnard* people toward the hamlet program is significantly different from that of the Vietnamese. In those parts of Vietnam inhabited by *montagnards*—more than twenty of the forty-three provinces have substantial *montagnard* populations—the implementation of the Strategic Hamlet Program was relatively easy. Unlike the lowland Vietnamese, who are very much attached to their traditional homes and especially to the ancestral graves nearby, the *montagnards* are essentially seminomadic, living in one clearing in the forest for a number of years and then, after the soil and game are exhausted, moving on to another location some miles away. While the typical Vietnamese prefers privacy, the mountain families band together in subtribal groups. In earlier days, this provided protection against raids from other tribes who came to take slaves; today it reflects habit and the bond of family and tribal association. Since the *montagnards* were already formed into hamlet-sized groups, and they customarily constructed high wooden fences around their camp sites as a barrier against marauding tigers, it only remained for the Vietnamese Government to provide them with additional materials for their fence, arm the village youth, and supply the trained health worker and other community improvements.

The typical Jarai house is built on stilts, six to eight feet above the ground. It is a dormitory-like structure, often twenty feet wide and a hundred feet long. Several related families often live in the same house; sometimes three generations are represented. The house is divided internally by bamboo screens, and has a springy floor of bamboo poles. The roof is made of thick thatch, the walls are of woven bamboo. Through the openings between the poles on the floor, scraps of refuse fall to the ground below and are immediately eaten by the hordes of dogs, chickens, and pigs who enjoy the cool shade underneath the house. Cooking and heating are done by a fire laid in a sandbox on the floor, and since no provisions are made for the smoke to escape, the inside of the dwelling is coated by a rich brown patina of wood smoke. The *montagnards* seem to retain this smoky smell, a not unpleasant odor rather like that of a well-cured ham. In fact, the smoke is used to cure ears of corn and slabs of fresh meat, which are hung near the fire until they have dried to rock hardness.

Huge earthen jars line the walls of a Jarai house; in these, the local wine, made of fermented rice or other grain, is brewed. A newly opened jar is activated by the addition of fresh water, and the wine that emerges is mild, with a tangy taste. A well-to-do *montagnard*, perhaps the tribal chief, will also have a number of large, round brass gongs, handed down from generation to generation. These are status symbols, in addition to their important role in tribal religious ceremonies. Sometimes they are exchanged as part of the purchase price for a new wife. They are expensive, a good gong often selling for the price of several water buffaloes.

Our morning-coffee conversation with Captain Stogner and Sergeant Garafolo was interrupted by the distant humming of a twin-engine airplane, which brought all of us out of the tent. The sharp-eyed sergeant identified it as a lumbering C-46 cargo plane, which, like the Jeep, was also a much-used veteran of World War II. The silver plane was headed in the direction of the Special Forces camp about five miles outside Cheo Reo, where it would make several low passes to alert the men that their supplies would be dropped. The plane would turn and circle above the airstrip, which was too short for it to land on, ready to drop the first supplies by parachutes. Captain Stogner was already piling into the Jeep, and it tore out the gate in a cloud of dust. The airstrip was close to our tents, so we had a front-row seat during every supply drop. A few minutes later, a truck, carrying some ten or fifteen young *montagnards* armed with submachine guns, roared by, heading for the airstrip. This was the recovery crew, whose duty was to spot and bring in the load of supplies about to descend on Cheo Reo. At one end of the dirt strip that served as the airport, Captain Stogner ignited a colored smoke grenade, a prearranged signal showing he was ready to receive the drop. This also helped the pilot to gauge the wind direction and velocity. The plane gunned its motors in acknowledgment, made one more lazy circle, and headed back over the airstrip at about 800 feet. Three bundles were kicked out of the open rear door of the plane in rapid succession and were brought up sharply as the red-and-white parachute canopies snapped open. The three chutes caught a fresh wind and drifted to the left of the airstrip. The pilot corrected his course and made a second, third, and fourth run, each time spewing out supplies like a spawning salmon. The recovery crews were waiting, and as a parachute-suspended bundle hit and bounced along the runway, the men quickly spilled the air from the chutes and detached the cargo containers. After a final pass, the plane banked sharply and began a tight climb back up to cruising altitude, out of range of possible guerrilla fire.

A little later, the truck and Jeep loaded with supplies passed by on the way back to the Special Forces camp. Sergeant Garafolo was holding a package carefully in his lap. The coffee had arrived.

There was still time to make my weekly economic check before the meeting at ten o'clock, so I picked up a notebook and walked down Tran Hung Dao Street to the marketplace. In all Vietnamese towns, the market is the center of life in the community. A multitude of small open-front shops surround the central square, where from dawn to sunset a pushing, shoving mass of itinerant peddlers, meat and fish hawkers, gossiping housewives, and pile after pile of fresh fruits and vegetables vie for the available space. Only a few of the vegetables and fruits would be recognizable in an American supermarket; bananas, coconuts, and limes perhaps, but the remainder are in shapes and sizes and colors completely foreign to the average American. *Montagnards* and Vietnamese alike mingled in the crowd, the Vietnamese making purchases in cash, the *montagnards* usually hoping to barter firewood, lumber, or perhaps some animal trapped in the forest. It was not at all unusual to see a huge python, a basket of chattering monkeys, or even an armored anteater being carried around by a *montagnard* hoping to make a favorable trade for colored cloth, beads, or a new ax.

In Phu Bon, as in other Highland provinces, there were two prices in the local market—one for the Vietnamese, and another, higher price for the *montagnards*. The mountain people had little real conception of money, and they were quickly separated from the small amount they earned. Since the local market was the only place where the products of the forest could be sold, they were at the mercy of the grasping businessman.

We considered the number of new shops built an indication of the local attitude toward the future of the province. A new store being constructed of cement or bricks, or with a metal roof gave evidence that the small businessman was in Phu Bon to stay. Such stores sprang up so quickly that I made a weekly count to keep abreast of the economic development. The recent addition of two small ice plants and a lumberyard greatly encouraged us, and one of my happiest moments was when I discovered that two Indian merchants had opened a tailor shop.

It took about one hour to make a survey of the market, and

then it was time for the meeting of the Provincial Committee. The meeting was to be held in Major Chi's office, at Provincial Headquarters. It was only a few hundred yards away, and I decided to walk. Last night's low of 50 degrees was only a distant memory as the hot tropical sun raised the temperature to the 90-degree mark. The double row of kapok trees lining the dirt road provided welcome shade. Only minimal activity was evident around the artillery positions as I passed. The daily chore of cleaning the big guns had already been completed. I passed a few *montagnards* on the way, driving a herd of brown-and-white goats ahead of them. Closer to headquarters, the sound of the field radio, still receiving messages from the outpost, was audible. The outpost served as the relay point for communication with the relief force, since their smaller backpacked radios were not strong enough to reach all the way to Cheo Reo.

When I reached headquarters, I found Major Will waiting in the anteroom, and an aide ushered us both into Major Chi's office. The office, like the rest of the rooms, was quite small. This building had been a district headquarters until Phu Bon was designated a new province. A large colored photograph of President Diem and a Vietnamese flag were the only wall decorations. Major Chi rose and, shaking hands, asked us to join him around the table. The aide brought in glasses of Vietnamese tea, lukewarm and amber-tinted, made with green tea leaves. At Major Chi's invitation, Major Will opened the meeting by listing the quantities of American-supplied barbed wire sent to the province for use in the Strategic Hamlet Program. He then discussed the supply of radios (provided by USOM), flashlights, and trip flares to be issued to the hamlet defenders after they had reached the proper stage of training.

Major Chi then took over. He explained that the lack of funds to pay provincial officials had reached the critical stage. Saigon had created the new province in September, but it had not yet provided him with any funds to administer it. The

military officers were getting paid, since their salaries came
from the army. But the clerks, typists, and officials of the
provincial technical services—health, education, public works,
etc.—were not receiving their salaries. This situation would
have caused a major scandal in the United States, or at least
a mass exodus of employees. The Vietnamese seemed to accept it with the fatalism born of experience. They had resorted
to borrowing from the local moneylenders at fantastic rates of
interest that would keep them in financial bondage for months
to come.

Their pay was now many months in arrears. The average
salary of a Vietnamese clerk or secretary is about 70 piasters
($1.00) per day. Housing is provided, usually (as in Phu Bon)
in a communal dormitory built of bamboo, sometimes with
only a dirt floor, and no electric lights or running water. Food
is cheap by American standards, a kilo (2⅕ lbs.) of rice cost-
ing about 10 cents. One kilo of rice is considered adequate for
three meals a day, when supplemented by soup or perhaps a
bit of chicken or pork. Working hours in the provincial offices
are from eight o'clock until five, with a break between twelve
and two.

After several comments on the slowness of the Saigon government, Major Chi got around to his proposal. He pointed
out that the joint U.S.-Vietnamese Provincial Rehabilitation
Agreement, a budget funded with U.S. money and designed
to support the newly created hamlet program, permitted the
hiring of a large number of workers to assist in projects such
as rebuilding houses and digging wells. Since only about thirty
hamlets were under construction, we had not hired the authorized number of people. Major Chi's request was that we
hire a number of local citizens and employ them in the provincial offices, paying them from the USOM budget, which
could be done at our discretion. The present civil servants
might continue to work without pay for some time, but it was
certain that no new applicant would appear. I could see his

point clearly. We had a new province, established in the middle of a wilderness without funds or trained people. The administration had to be kept going or the whole effort would collapse. A long discussion ensued as we explored possible solutions. Seeing that he had our sympathy, Major Chi loaded his biggest gun and fired it in my direction.

"You know we have many refugee people at Boun Ba Mala, in Phu Tuc District. But I have no one to distribute properly the many good things USOM sends to us. I have no one to keep watch over the supplies and look after the refugees. Why can't we use the USOM money to hire men for this job?"

His logic was clear. We had a problem. We had money. Why not use the money to solve the problem? How to translate this into pay for the much-needed civil servants was another question. Major Will made a suggestion: Why not detail soldiers for the job? Major Chi explained why this was not feasible, but the word "detail" stuck in our minds. Why not hire workers under the Rehabilitation Agreement and "detail" them to the refugee camps and provincial offices? It was done. The Provincial Committee, with the flexibility and resources that were designed to support the new concept of decentralized government, had proved its worth again. It just happened that the workers hired under this plan had qualifications that fitted them to be schoolteachers, health workers, typists, truck drivers, and supervisors. I began to regain confidence in the real usefulness of direct U.S. aid, confidence I had lost the night before when our help seemed useless in the face of a Viet Cong attack.

At Major Chi's request, I summarized the total input of USOM refugee assistance to Phu Bon. Our program was based on the following: We estimated the total population of Phu Bon Province at about 55,000. Of these, 47,000 were living in areas controlled by the government. Most of these—42,000—were *montagnards*, chiefly Jarai, but including substantial numbers of Trung, Bahnar, and M'dur. The remaining 5,000 were

Vietnamese. Since military security was provided by a special
operation that began three months ago, 18,000 refugees had requested assistance from the government, and 11,000 were still
in three refugee centers. The other 7,000 had already been resettled in strategic hamlets.

From the U.S. standpoint, 11 million piasters, or about
$165,000, had been allocated to the province for refugee relief
and resettlement. The bulk of this amount, 6 million piasters,
was for the purchase of rice and dried fish; the remainder for
new tools, seeds, blankets, and salaries for hamlet workers. In
addition to the official funds, I had asked for and received
from USOM in Saigon more than 2,000 bags of wheat, 360
bags of corn, 280 bags of beans, 275 bags of cement, and almost 3,000 heavy new shirts for distribution to the refugees.

Just then the aide dashed in, asking Major Chi and Major
Will to come to the outer room. One of the Americans accompanying the relief force at the outpost was sending a message
on the radio through his Vietnamese interpreter. Major Chi
gave a running translation as the sound of the radio filled the
small room. The relief force had arrived at the hamlet and
found it, not in ruins or under siege as we had feared, but in a
state of alcoholic oblivion! Every man, woman, and child
seemed to be sleeping off the effects of a gigantic hangover.
The sober souls were the owners of several buffaloes, which
seemed to have been killed by artillery fire the night before
as they grazed quietly in the moist grass of a nearby pasture.
After somewhat ungentlemanly prodding, the groggy Hamlet
Chief admitted that a tribal ceremony had been in full swing
the night before, climaxed, after too many trips to the wine
jug, by a mass firing of weapons into the night sky. Seeing the
rather ominous expressions on the faces of the tired and angry
soldiers, the chief hastened to add that the ceremony had been
in honor of the Vietnamese and Americans who had provided
the hamlet with such fine weapons. There was some confusion
at the other end of the radio as the American adviser gave vent

to some short and rather pithy comments about the whole situation. Apparently his interpreter had not been taught the exact Vietnamese translation of these expressions, but we got the message.

Major Chi was very angry at this waste of artillery and manpower, and his face flushed as he made ready to order drastic punishment for the offenders. Major Will and I quickly pointed out that the only casualties were a few buffaloes. With some bad luck, the artillery could have wiped out half the hamlet. Somewhat mollified, Major Chi returned to the conference room.

The remainder of the meeting was taken up with the multitude of minor details that had to be discussed and agreed upon so that funds could be spent. Major Chi reminded us of the *montagnard* ceremony in the afternoon. This ended the meeting of the Provincial Committee, and I left for my next appointment.

A short Jeep ride took me to the only Phu Bon weather station, at the home of the French priest. Of all the individuals I met in Vietnam, he was one of the most unusual. There were two French missionary priests in Phu Bon, one who ministered to the needs of the Vietnamese Catholic population and the other who concerned himself solely with the *montagnards*. The former was a stocky bearded man, who had been a prisoner of the Chinese Communists. He built a new church, school, and orphanage in Phu Bon, and the Vietnamese nuns under his supervision also staffed the provincial hospital. He was a jolly man of considerable stature in the community.

The other, whom I was going to see, presented a great contrast. He was tall, very thin, and had a dour expression. The round, jolly priest had a crew cut and wore the brown robe of a monk; the *montagnard* priest—everyone called him that— had a shock of tumbled hair and usually wore Levi trousers with a wide leather belt and no shirt. On his bare chest hung the only outward symbol of his calling, a crude hand-carved cross. He lived alone in a Jarai long house, built in a secluded spot off the main street of Cheo Reo. To reach his door required a climb up the shaky wooden ladder traditional among the mountain people. Another long house, connected to his living quarters by a covered elevated passageway, served as his chapel. Inside the father's house was a collection of books and paintings, looking somehow out of place in the otherwise conventional *montagnard* dwelling. It was only later that I learned that in a curtained-off portion of the house he had a small dispensary set up where he cared for the sick and injured. The traditional wine jar of the Jarai was nowhere in evidence, and his only vice seemed to be his pipe.

Despite my small personal contribution of money and several offers of assistance to his people, he never relaxed or unbent in the slightest. A man of few words, he made his longest speech one day when he lectured me on the futility of my trying to improve the *montagnards'* agricultural methods. He recalled that the French had tried the same thing in this area for many years. As long as the French adviser had remained, the *montagnards* used the new techniques. But as soon as he left, they went back to their old ways. I had reason to remember this bit of advice many times.

On this occasion, after a few words of greeting, he grudgingly agreed to give me the weather information I wanted. By now, it was almost time for the arrival of Dr. Voulgaropoulos and Joe Haritani. I thanked the priest and bade him good-by. I could not help seeing the relief in his eyes as I started down the ladder, leaving him once again in peace in his own small world.

On the way to the airstrip, I thought about our relations with the more conventional elements of the U.S. Operations Mission in Vietnam. The formation of the Rural Affairs Office had not been met with great enthusiasm by the old-time AID men in Vietnam. They had, up to this point, considered their jobs to consist essentially in advising their Vietnamese associates within the city limits of Saigon. The separate world of the provinces had not yet become a reality to them. After the first few weeks in Phu Bon, I had begun to realize that the local problems were far beyond my limited capabilities. The province needed help from experts, and needed it badly. So, taking a map of the province and the vivid impression of 11,000 *montagnard* refugees living in fly-infested camps, I had hurried back to Saigon several weeks before and made the rounds of the various technical divisions in USOM. I visited the offices of health, public works, education, agriculture, and the rest. At each stop, I opened my map, spread out some photographs, and made a sales pitch. Reactions varied according to the individual and his concept of his job.

In the USOM Division of Public Health, I found a willing ear and a kindred spirit in Dr. Emmanuel Voulgaropoulos, a good-looking young doctor who had served with Dr. Tom Dooley in Laos and Cambodia. Dr. "Vee" (as he was called by the Vietnamese, who could never pronounce his full name) had married an attractive American woman, Rose, while working in the wilds of Cambodia. Later he joined the U.S. Public Health Service and AID in Vietnam. Dr. Vee disliked Saigon desk life and took every opportunity to travel throughout the countryside. Within a matter of days, he fitted a trip to Phu Bon into his busy schedule.

Less than six months after my first meeting with Dr. Vee, the whole USOM advisory effort seemed to pick up speed—urged, coaxed, and prodded by the Provincial Representatives in the provinces and the Rural Affairs staff in Saigon—and it geared up for the war. Today, the presence of large numbers of technical-division advisers in the rural areas is so common as to go without mention, but in the fall of 1962, even a one-hour trip by air to Phu Bon provided enough color for several evenings of cocktail conversation in Saigon. But Dr. Vee was an exception even then, and cocktail small talk had no part in his plans.

The purpose of his visit today was to plan a joint U.S.-Vietnamese health campaign to vaccinate the refugees against smallpox and determine which had contracted malaria.

Almost at the appointed minute, the little twin-engine blue-and-white Cessna appeared over the airstrip and buzzed the American tents. I parked my beat-up old Willys Jeep and was waiting when the plane landed. With Dr. Vee was Joe Haritani, a Japanese-American with a million-dollar personality and a good mind. The wives of Dr. Vee and Joe had sent up some ice cream and a homemade cake, which were well received and rapidly eaten.

We got into details of the planned health operation immediately, since both men had additional stops to make before darkness closed in. The health problems of the *montagnard* people were of a kind only read about in modern America. Infectious diseases such as the plague, typhoid, cholera, and malaria were commonplace in the Highlands. While each isolated group of refugees might have built up an immunity to certain diseases, the mass movement into one central location, combined with overcrowed conditions, opened up the possibilities of a real epidemic. In addition, savage attacks by tigers and the bites of cobras and kraits were a daily occurrence in Phu Bon. Many of the young *montagnards* were gored by buffaloes, after the animals had been tormented by thoughtless children. This province of 55,000 people had no doctor and only a few trained nurses. Solving its health problems would require a massive effort. That was exactly the kind of effort that Dr. Vee and Joe were proposing, and subsequently mounted. Dr. Vee promised that tons of medical supplies and large numbers of Vietnamese technicians would be flown into the province. He made good on his promise, chiefly through his personal intervention with his Vietnamese medical friends in the Ministry of Health in Saigon. My part in this program would be to determine as closely as possible the number and location of all the refugee camps, then handle ground transportation from the Cheo Reo airstrip to the camps. I was to persuade the Civil Guard to provide some trucks, drivers, and an unloading crew in exchange for whatever "extra" medical supplies we might have. Since the health operation would last a number of days, there also would be a storage problem for supplies; I would have to manage to borrow space in a local warehouse by judicious horse-trading. The province was ill-prepared to provide even temporary housing for the incoming medical workers, and I would have to spend the best part of a day locating suitable quarters. The Vietnamese tend to be somewhat disorganized in these matters; when the big U.S. Air Force C-123 cargo planes did come in with the medical supplies, I and several other Americans ended up unloading most of them ourselves. But the most significant improvement was the response of the Vietnamese Ministry of Health.

With their final plans made, Dr. Vee and Joe climbed back aboard the Cessna. The pilot held the little ship on the ground until it seemed that they must have gone past the runway, then pulled up sharply, and was soon out of sight beyond the hills guarding our river valley. After lunch, I was ready for the afternoon siesta and whatever the *montagnard* ceremony would bring.

At a quarter of three, we were waiting at the hamlet for the beginning of the ceremony. Major Chi would arrive a few minutes later, upholding the dignity of his office. This important ceremony was to be the occasion of the swearing of allegiance to President Ngo Dinh Diem and the Government of Vietnam. Diem was favorably regarded by the *montagnards*, since he had spent several years as a District Chief in a province with a *montagnard* population. The ritual of fealty was to be carried out according to the custom of the mountain people.

Every *montagnard* chief in the district of Thuan Man was assembled. Waiting for Major Chi's arrival were Major Will and his staff, all looking very military in clean, pressed fatigues, shined boots, and fresh shaves; the entire Special Forces Team, everyone surprisingly enough wearing the same uniform and, of course, a green beret. The top echelon of the Phu Bon Civil Service were present also, attired in long-sleeved white shirts with French cuffs, ties, dark trousers, and pointed-toe leather shoes.

Inside the hamlet, I could hear the gong-bearers giving tentative taps to their instruments and the voices of excited children. The hamlet gate was arched over with festive banners and brightly flapping Vietnamese flags. A wide path had been laid directly to the large pavilion constructed in the center of the hamlet. Much to my consternation, the pavilion appeared to have been built with shining new sheets of roofing that could have come only from the USOM stockpile intended for the Strategic Hamlet Program. I made a mental note to discuss this with Major Chi at the first opportunity.

The pavilion was gaily decked with cloth bunting of red and yellow, the Vietnamese national colors. In front of the stand was a sturdy flagpole from whose tip flew the Vietnamese flag. A table at the base of the pole held a large portrait of President Diem, surrounded by vases of fresh wild flowers. A very colorful scene in the otherwise drab hamlet.

Standing in formation along the path were a double rank of *montagnard* soldiers acting as the honor guard. Many were barefoot or wore loincloths in place of trousers, but the submachine guns at their sides testified to their profession.

The center of interest seemed to be the five huge water buffaloes, each tied to a separate pole in front of the pavilion. The buffaloes, usually very quiet and patient animals, were restless and fretful, obviously bothered by the noise and excitement. Small boys were running up and jabbing at them with sticks, or throwing stones at the heads of the helpless beasts.

A thousand tribespeople, neatly formed into groups of fifty

by age and sex, were lined up along the path. The men were
on the left side, the women and children on the right. The
men were dressed in loincloths and long-sleeved black hand-
woven shirts decorated in front with red beads and piping. The
women were wearing formal attire, which unfortunately included blouses as well as their customary skirts. The blouses
were of black hand-woven cotton, with wide horizontal red
stripes. The almost uniform-like sameness of the *montagnards'*
dress emphasized the distinction between them and the Vietnamese.

Major Chi arrived in his Jeep, a highly polished model with
white seat covers. He made a point of personally greeting each
of the guests. Then, with erect carriage and expressionless face,
he strode through the hamlet gate. The ceremony was under
way.

The commander of the honor guard called his unit to attention and presented arms. Their speed and precision might
not have won the approval of a West Point drill instructor,
but not the slightest smile crossed the faces of the American
military advisers.

With Major Chi leading the way, we walked up the path.
As our party passed in front of each group of *montagnards,*
they gave three reasonably enthusiastic cheers, thrusting their
right arms with fists clenched skyward. It looked like a Cecil
B. De Mille movie of the return of Julius Caesar to Rome. The
emotional impact of one of these "triumphal entries" is very
great. One gets an almost irresistible impulse to nod grandly
to the crowd and smooth a nonexistent toga or laurel wreath.

The party reached the pavilion and took its place on the
stand. Major Chi, Major Will, and I were awarded the center
of the front row; the other officials were seated according to
some form of protocol.

The crowd quieted down, and, as at any ceremony any-
where, the speeches began. The first speech, of course by Major Chi, was translated into the Jarai dialect by a *montagnard*

boy who had been educated in a Vietnamese school. Very few Vietnamese officials bother to learn the tribal languages; in Phu Bon, only one highly motivated District Chief, a young lieutenant, spent the time necessary to master the guttural sounds.

After the speeches were finished, three venerable old men came forward, their lined faces and white hair heightening the dignity of the ceremony. They were clad in bright flowing silk tunics of red and black, slit up the sides to show white trousers beneath. These men represented important figures in the Jarai religion: the King of Fire, the King of Water, and the King of the Wind.. According to the *montagnard* religion, which is animistic, ordinary objects contain spirits, some evil and some good. The flowing stream has a spirit, the strangely shaped rock or tree in the forest may be known for miles around as the abiding place of a special demon. The three old Kings, or priests, were the representatives of the spirits that lived in three elements important to life—air, fire, and water.

The old men moved to the front of the pavilion and arranged themselves before a row of large earthen jars, the traditional wine containers of the Jarai. Each jar contained a bamboo drinking straw. The three priests poured fresh water from a gourd into the wine jars until they were brimful. Then, beginning with Major Chi, we each went forward and sat down on chairs placed in front of the wine jars. The King of Fire indicated we were to remove one shoe and stocking. The bare foot was then placed on an unsheathed ax head lying on the ground. The priests began a low, repetitive chanting in Jarai, counting from one to seven, and then invoking the curse of all evil spirits on our heads if we should ever break this bond of friendship with the Jarai people. All the while, the brass gongs were sounding softly in the background. A hush had fallen over the entire assembly as the priests performed their rites. Finally, wine from the large jars was siphoned up through the straw and allowed to trickle over our bare feet.

When this was completed, pretty young Jarai girls placed a bracelet of thick brass wire on our wrists. This indicated that we had participated in the ceremony and had an eternal bond of friendship and pact of peace with the Jarai people. These bracelets are worn with pride and just a hint of superstition by those who have served in the Highlands, and it is not unusual to find an entire Special Forces Team wearing these bracelets with the pride usually reserved only for their famous green berets.

When this part of the ceremony was completed, Major Chi responded for the Vietnamese Government. I had agreed to provide Major Chi with USOM goods to be given to the *montagnards* during the ceremony. They would be a symbol of the tons of materials already flown in from Saigon and distributed through the refugee centers to the *montagnards*.

Bashful young men and women representing all the hamlets in the district now came forward to receive a gift; each was given a new shirt, farming tools, and a sack of bulgur wheat by an equal number of self-conscious visitors who had left the stand to present the gifts formally. Above the large stack of gifts, Major Chi had erected a banner acknowledging the assistance of the United States to the Vietnamese people.

It had been difficult from the start to restrain Major Chi from giving public credit to the U.S. Government. I explained that our objective was to assist the Vietnamese Government to win the support of its own people. My job was to help build up this rapport between the people and Viet Nam Cong Hoa —the Government of the Republic of Vietnam. That was why we gave the materials to Major Chi, so that he himself could give them to the people. Being Vietnamese, and therefore a practical man, Major Chi found it difficult to believe that we did not want publicity. Why should we provide material things to the Vietnamese Government so that the Vietnamese *montagnards* would like their own government and not ours? I think he really felt we were just being polite and insisted all the more on having banners painted with slogans about the gratitude of the Vietnamese people for this assistance. I, myself, sometimes felt a little foolish trying to convince him he should not mention the American Government. We finally compromised on a sort of "people-to-people" agreement, whereby he stated that the American people felt sympathy for the Vietnamese people in their struggle against the Viet Cong, and wanted to help.

The ceremony was now reaching its climax. At a signal from one of the priests, there was a flurry of activity around each of the five buffaloes. Young men with spears and axes hacked away at the hind legs of the buffaloes as if they were cutting trees in the forest. The bloody axes bit deeply into the rear tendons of the animals, while the spearmen thrust their weapons into the heaving flanks, seeking the heart. One by one, the lumbering beasts crumpled to the ground, bellowing in pain and fear. One of the leaders stepped forward with an empty tin basin. He held it below the sagging head of the nearest buffalo, catching the blood pouring from the mouth of the dying animal. As the last buffalo collapsed and died, a great shout went up from the *montagnards*. There would be fresh meat for all.

The basin of warm blood was brought to the front of the pavilion. The priests began dipping a number of chipped and dirty glasses into the basin, half filling them. Then they poured an equal measure of rice wine into the blood-filled glasses. Major Chi, looking a little green himself, grasped my arm and led me to the ceremonial table. I began to realize that my diplomatic abilities were about to receive their greatest test. Swearing vengeance on my fellow USOM friends who had pre-empted the assignments to the comfortable Mekong Delta, where the only problem was the Viet Cong, I reflected that here I could be eaten by tigers, trampled by elephants, bitten by snakes, and even have the distinction of being the only USOM adviser to live in a tent. Before common sense or my churning stomach could prevail, I downed the cloudy mixture in one long gulp. The other Americans followed suit, and for once even the Special Forces Team looked a little apprehensive. Finally, the *montagnard* chiefs had their glass of wine and blood, which they seemed to drink with relish.

Then came the most solemn act of the ritual. Each man walked to the table and picked up one of the three weapons lying there, a knife, an ax, or a modern submachine gun, and held it to his lips. Major Chi explained that this was a very old custom among the *montagnards* by which they swore eternal loyalty to a leader. As each man picked up one of the weapons, he vowed to die by this same weapon if he ever betrayed his oath. The only variation from the ancient traditions of this ceremony was the addition of the modern gun—a reminder of the vicious guerrilla war being waged today.

The ceremony was now completed. There was a general shaking of hands, and we walked back down the path to the same accompaniment of cheers and gong-ringing. No sooner had our Jeeps left the gate than all the *montagnards*, men, women, children, and soldiers alike, broke ranks and ran toward the buffaloes. They would cook them as they lay, building a huge wood fire around each animal. By nightfall, the feast would be ready, the outside of the buffaloes charred and blackened, the inside steam-cooked. The intestines, liver, and heart would be served up as choice bits to the leaders and children. By morning, only piles of broken bones would remain.

On the way back to our compound, Major Will signaled for a stop at the *cau lac bo*, literally "assembly building" or "meeting place," in Vietnamese. The *cau lac bo* was just across the road from our compound, at a much-traveled intersection. When we first came to Phu Bon, it was an empty building through which cows and pigs frequently roamed. Then some enterprising Vietnamese businessman had patched up the holes, put in a cement floor, added tables and a small bar, and imported five young hostesses. They served beer, Coke, and lunch to tired businessmen. A tiny record player, some fluorescent lights, and a few pin-ups from old American magazines completed the fittings. It was the only place for recreation for American and Vietnamese officials in the whole province. Once Major Will had requested Dr. Voulgaropoulos to make a health survey of the *cau lac bo*. He found that the dishes were washed in cold water, the food was prepared on a ground-level stone slab, and the girls were of doubtful virtue. Still, it was the only place in the province, so Major Will placed everything in the establishment off limits to Americans except the bottled beverages.

Major Chi was coaxed into joining us, and after a few drinks, dropped his usual reserve and soon joined in singing a few French songs. For a while, the war was forgotten, even by the Vietnamese who had been fighting it for twenty years.

After dinner that evening, Major Will brought out a 16-mm. movie projector and an American feature film provided by the army. We invited Major Chi and his staff, who arrived with their shy wives and eager children. Our gasoline-driven generator soon had the latest Hollywood production flashing across the screen, and the mess sergeant even produced some popcorn. After the movie, everyone turned in for a good night's rest.

Soon the generator was shut off and our three tents were plunged into darkness. There was nothing to do but sleep. Months later, when a permanent compound was built and electricity was available all night, I used the evening hours to write up the multitude of reports that we were obliged to turn out. But now, in the quiet darkness, I could think back over the day's accomplishments and frustrations.

It is difficult being an adviser in Asia; every instinct shouts for immediate personal intervention whenever some seemingly logical and necessary project gets shunted off into oblivion because it conflicts with a local religious, political, or purely personal interest. Americans by tradition and inclination seem much better fitted to get things done themselves than hopefully offer advice to others. Here in Phu Bon there were not enough Vietnamese officials to do the work, even if they were all efficient and dedicated. The important agriculture service and farmers' small loan service (the National Agricultural Credit Organization) were nonexistent. The public-works section did not even have a wooden road drag, much less a bulldozer or other mechanized equipment. But on the positive side, Major Chi was beginning to agree to some of the ideas I presented; among them, a special training center to teach the *montagnards* proper methods of planting and irrigation, a special school program to make primary education available throughout the province. And, most astonishing of all, the Provincial Medical Chief had even agreed to put screens on the doors and windows of the twelve-bed hospital. Perhaps later he might be convinced that only one patient should be placed in each bed and that those with tuberculosis should not be placed next to newborn infants. It was going to be a long uphill fight in Phu Bon. On this uncertain note, I drifted off to sleep.

The roar of artillery fire brought me awake for the second time in twenty-four hours. I looked at my watch. It was almost midnight. I thought for a moment: "This is where I came in. I wonder how many water buffaloes we'll have to pay for this time." Then I rolled over and went back to sleep.

4

QUANG NAM PROVINCE

by

WILLIAM A. NIGHSWONGER

THE SEAPORT OF DA NANG is in the heart of Central Vietnam
—a three-day drive from Saigon up Highway 1. Flying time is
about two hours across the vast Highland plateau, home of a
half-million non-Vietnamese tribal peoples. Or you can take a
little longer, following the magnificent coastline, passing the
wet jungles east of Saigon, and skimming the dry coastal provinces, which have only a few inches of rainfall a year. Halfway
up the coast, you see the idyllic resort and harbor city of Nha-
trang. Here you enter Central Vietnam, in many ways a different world from the south.

Whatever the season of the year, the weather will be the
exact opposite of that in Saigon. From Phu Yen Province to
the 17th parallel, it rains heavily from September through
March; the Saigon monsoon begins in the spring and continues to the fall. The terrain is also different in Central Vietnam. A half-dozen rivers along some 400 miles of coastline
nourish a heavily populated strip of farming lowland that sep-
arates the sea from the Annamite Mountains, where the tribal

peoples live. These communities themselves are different—settled centuries earlier than those in the south—more like China.

When your aircraft reaches Da Nang, you have already passed over two-thirds of Central Vietnam. In front of you to the north, overlooking the South China Sea, is the formidable Ai Van Pass, where Highway 1 threads its way through the mountains to Hué, terminating at the border with North Vietnam. South Vietnam is at its narrowest point at the pass, which is less than fifty miles from the Lao border, with only jungles and mountains between.

The city of Da Nang and the big U.S. jet base nestle at the mouth of the Thu Bon River, with the ocean on the east, the bay to the north, and foothills directly west along the edge of the air base. Networks of U.S. Marine defenses on these hills guard the base and act as a buffer to the imposing mountains farther west, which are under the rule of the Viet Cong night and day.

Da Nang is an independent city of 150,000, at the northeast tip of Quang Nam Province. You can see the whole of the province in less than an hour by helicopter. Let us take the trip.

Rising swiftly from the runway, we follow Highway 1 below us, and proceed south. Six miles on our left are the beach and three stumpy, stony protrusions called Marble Mountain, with its astonishing varieties of marble and its little community of carvers.

As far as we can see to the south is a myriad of hamlets, clusters of houses fenced with rows of live bamboo and surrounded by rice paddies. Adjoining the hamlets are burial areas, dotted with circular earthen tombs—the villager's sacred tie to his ancestors.

In a few minutes, toward the sea on the left, we see the broad mouth of the Thu Bon River. Nearby is the province capital of Hoi An. For a thousand years, this city, until recently called Faifo, has perched on the edge of the river, a meeting place for sampans from the interior—loaded with cinnamon, precious woods, silk—and traders from China, Japan, India, and, more recently, Europe.

As we reach the river, we turn away from the sea and the city and move west, up the river, into the interior of the province. Like a great horn of plenty, the broad delta narrows during the scant twenty minutes it takes by chopper to reach the end of the valley. From the air, on a clear day, you can see from one end of the valley to the other.

Along the banks of this river, 400,000 people live, and another 100,000 on its tributaries. We are looking down on the highest concentration of population in rural South Vietnam: 2,000 persons per square mile. Most of the villages apportion their lands yearly in equal amounts to each voter, with the average family holding about half an acre.

Since there is not enough land to sustain the people, Quang Nam Province imports about 20,000 tons of rice yearly from the richer Mekong Delta. And the people have had to find ways to augment their farm income. Beneath the thatch roofs that line the riverbanks are 4,000 hand looms turning out cotton cloth.

Just a mile off Highway 1, we can still find a complete cottage-industry cycle in a single village. One hamlet grows silkworms and the mulberry leaves to feed them, a second hamlet reels the silk from the cocoons, and a third hamlet has looms that weave silk into cloth and tiny fish nets. Once many looms produced fine silks, but now the silk market is largely gone, lost to the Japanese and the Thais.

The Thu Bon River is the heartbeat of these half-million Vietnamese. But it can also be a heartbreak. In November, 1964, perhaps the worst flood in its history engulfed the whole valley for days. At least 3,000 people were drowned. Some 60,000 domestic animals died. Hundreds of people died of food poisoning after eating the only food they had: the bloated bodies of dead animals. When it rains in Quang Nam, it really rains; in one eighteen-hour period, there were eighteen inches of rain. And in a whole month during the flood, there were three hours of sunlight.

As the valley narrows, a tributary appears on the left between two mountains. Here, fifteen centuries ago, the Hindu Champa kings built a majestic capital city, My Son. Its ruins are still there, although the site is reportedly used by the Viet Cong as a field hospital.

Farther up this tributary, we can see the outlines of the An Hoa industrial complex, with plans for diversified industrial investments totaling $40 million. A few miles beyond, at Nong Son, is the only producing coal mine in South Vietnam; this is the energy and raw-materials source for the industrial complex.

Passing the confluence of the tributary and the main river, we follow the big river due west. At the jungle's edge, we can see the village of An Diem, the westernmost point of Vietnamese habitation. On three sides are looming mountains, home of the xenophobic Katu Highland tribe—and the Viet Cong. The Katu inhabit the thirty-five miles of territory up to the Lao border, vital entry points of the Ho Chi Minh Trail. Forty-three of the Katu, mostly old women and children, live in An Diem, in the care of a Vietnamese Protestant pastor. Some 8,000 others have been moved by the Viet Cong deep into the mountainous jungles to bear arms, raise crops, and be guides along the Ho Chi Minh Trail.

Perhaps the most isolated of Vietnamese tribal groups, the Katu were not controlled by the French until the 1930's. Their bitterness at French repression, and the cheating of Vietnamese merchants with whom they traded cinnamon and betel, made them receptive to Vietminh persuasion. Key young men were taken to North Vietnam for training in 1954 and returned to assist the Viet Cong in using the tribe for Communist purposes.

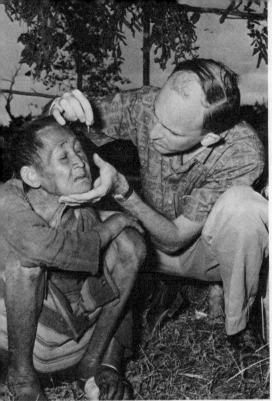

Earl Young provides
medical assistance to a
refugee

Major Pham Dinh Chi, Chief of Province, Phu Bon

Doctor "Vee" of the Phu Bon health operation

Sacks of flour presented
to the *montagnards* in
Phu Bon

Quang Nam Province: inhabited highland is surrounded by paddies

William Nighswonger visits remote hamlet by boat

Farmers at Phu Nam Tay relocate their homes inside the fence

Children in school in Thuong Duc; the building and books were furnished by U.S. AID

And so you have seen it all by air in only a few minutes—the whole of Quang Nam, a microcosm of Central Vietnamese life on a single river, the home of half a million hardy peasant people.

The complex contribution of China to Quang Nam's religious life, transmitted during a thousand years of Chinese domination, includes Buddhism, Taoism, and Confucianism. The dividing lines between these systems are not clear in China, nor are they clear in Quang Nam. One may, indeed, be both a Buddhist and a Confucian, and most of the pagodas embody a mixture of several religious traditions. Nearly every peasant home has a shelf serving as an altar to the family's forefathers, with candlesticks, an incense holder, and perhaps a picture of an eminent ancestor. Buddhist bonzes (priests) can be found here and there in the countryside, but places of worship far outnumber professional clergy.

Catholicism has had vigorous representation in Quang Nam for several centuries, but its adherents amount to only 5 per cent of the population. Protestants and members of the Cao Dai sect together account for 1 per cent.

Rivalry and resentment between Catholics and non-Catholics are deep in the traditions of the province. Under President Diem, Catholics were favored for government posts. Most non-Catholics identified with the Buddhists, as they do now. In the summer of 1963, the Quang Nam Province Chief, a former intelligence officer and a devout Catholic, appointed a committee of trusted members of the Can Lao (a semi-secret Diemist organization of public officials) to help dispose of the Buddhist problems. In July, Buddhist discontents erupted in a demonstration near the pagoda in Hoi An in which twenty-five were wounded. Guards were then placed at all major pagodas, and the people stopped attending them. Despite the largely Buddhist face of the Saigon government since the overthrow of Diem, in November, 1963, tension between religious communities continues in Quang Nam and other provinces.

The government in the province follows the general Vietnamese pattern. The Province Chief is the senior civil administrator and the military commander in Quang Nam. He reports militarily to the division commander in Da Nang and, as a civilian, to the Minister of the Interior in Saigon. The Province Chief is responsible for coordinating the work of twenty provincial departments, most of which are also under ministries in Saigon. These departments include: Police, Public Works, Education, Public Health, Information, Tax, Youth, etc.

There are nine districts whose chiefs report to the Province Chief. These districts range in population from 17,000 to 95,-000. There are 120 villages, most of them with a council and a Village Chief elected by the people. Each village has several hamlets, and there are more than 500 hamlets in the province. Taxes and lawsuits begin at the village level; it is the lowest legal structure and traditionally has had considerable political autonomy. For many rural Vietnamese, the village is the only government they know. It is the primary social and political unit with which they identify, beyond the extended family itself.

With the reluctant assent of the village notables, the territory of Quang Nam Province was divided in 1962, the lower one-third becoming a new province, Quang Tin. Until then, Quang Nam had been the largest province in Vietnam—and one of the proudest. The lowlands of the province are separated from Hué by the Ai Van Pass, and the mountains almost divide Quang Tin on the south from Quang Ngai Province below it. This isolation has developed strong local loyalties.

The province has always been a political hotbed. The Vietnamese refer to it as the "province of contention." The Province Chief receives about fifty letters and petitions a week on various local matters—a large number for a Vietnamese province.

Quang Nam is the center of the Vietnam Quoc Dan Dang (Nationalist Party), whose name parallels that of the Chinese Kuomintang (or Nationalist People's Party). Long a revolutionary quasi-secret group that opposed the French, Japanese, and Diem, the Quoc Dan Dang was assisted by the Chinese in earlier decades. Today it is divided and weakened as a result of close surveillance in the Diem period and competition from the Viet Cong. Nevertheless, it represents the only substantial political organization in the villages apart from the Communists.

Quang Nam has produced many Communist revolutionaries. Several top leaders in the North and in the Southern Liberation Front are from this province. Its recently dismembered territory, now Quang Tin Province, has also long been a center of considerable Viet Cong strength.

The Viet Cong limited most of their lowland activity during 1960–63 to isolated incidents of terror and assassination and to continued political propaganda and recruiting efforts. After the fall of Diem, the pattern remained largely the same, except that recruiting and terror were stepped up and a perceptible move developed from the Viet Cong mountain bases toward the sea. By the end of 1964, the Viet Cong were conducting propaganda and military operations in all the lowlands. They had begun to destroy the railroad and major bridges on Highway 1.

The Viet Cong approach to villagers in Quang Nam focuses on local issues through the Quang Nam Liberation Front, run completely by the Viet Cong. On occasion, a village chief may be executed for corruption. Control over the villages apparently reaches to within shouting distance of the Da Nang air base. After sighting a Viet Cong flag in a village, government pilots bombed the village school, killing about twenty adults and children. The citizens marched with the bodies of their dead to the air base to protest. The Viet Cong often have such ready-made issues, and they usually exploit them brilliantly.

According to the best estimates, the Viet Cong regular forces in Quang Nam have trebled in the past year, and they provide a powerful, persuasive basis for psychological operations.

Realizing the danger posed by existing and threatened Viet Cong operations in Quang Nam Province, the Vietnamese Government joined with the United States in concentrated efforts to pacify the province. The first phase, lasting from 1962 to 1963, centered on the Strategic Hamlet Program. Patterned after the Malayan experiment that had helped bring success against Communist terrorists, this program had been under way for six months when I was assigned by USOM to be Provincial Representative in Quang Nam. Scores of hamlets had the bamboo fences and other outward marks of the strategic hamlet. But little money or manpower had been made available until the launching of the USOM Provincial Rehabilitation Agreements, which were just being written.

Sixty hamlets in Quang Nam had already been listed by the province government as "completed," that is, having satisfied six criteria: defenses built, people organized for civil-defense tasks, militia trained and armed, Viet Cong agents named and isolated, hamlet elections held, and a secret "stay behind" friendly guerrilla cell organized.

An agreement designed to finance the Quang Nam Province program had been drawn up by a joint Government of Vietnam–U.S. team that visited the province in November, 1962. The agreement authorized the establishment of a three-man Provincial Rehabilitation Committee composed of the Vietnamese Province Chief, the senior U.S. Military Sector Adviser, and the USOM Provincial Representative. The committee was responsible for authorizing all expenditures and certifying all receipts. The Province Chief was the project manager, responsible for carrying out the decisions of the committee. Although it was understood that most proposals would necessarily come from the Province Chief and his staff—with veto power over finances in the hands of the U.S. representatives—suggestions from the U.S. side were frequent.

As the USOM Representative, my main job was to see that the program of action agreed on by Americans and Vietnamese at the national level proceeded properly and effectively at the province level. We were, as a committee, free to adjust allocations of money in the agreement up to 20 per cent of the totals. Fortunately, a sizable "miscellaneous" fund, equal to about 10 per cent of the budget, was available for unanticipated expenses. This was drawn on often.

The goals for the nationwide Strategic Hamlet Program went far beyond the primary objective of separating and protecting the rural people from the Viet Cong. The larger purpose was to build a new image of the government in the minds of the people, by increasing the services of government—providing better schools, health workers, agricultural assistance—at the village level. The people were encouraged to express their will in the election of their own Hamlet Committee and in the choice of a self-help project to benefit the whole community. (Money and materials were to be supplied by the province via the Rehabilitation Agreement.) In short, the hamlet program was supposed to produce a genuine transformation in rural life, a revolution bringing social, economic, and political fulfillment.

We concentrated our first efforts in Quang Nam on about forty hamlets surrounding the An Hoa industrial complex. Formed as a new district for the campaign, the area was given highest national priority in hamlet-building and was run directly by the Vietnamese Army Division Commander, instead of by the Province Chief. The area had a long record of Viet Cong influence, from the earliest days of the Vietminh, and was in close touch with the Viet Cong. In contrast, the

successful Malayan program was based on fortifying secure
areas first, working gradually outward to the less secure areas,
in the well-known oil-spot technique.

The ambitious young Division Commander rapidly revised
his timetable to impress President Diem, cutting the comple-
tion date from a projected six months down to three and,
finally, to two and a half months.

The Province Chief was required to supply about fifty civil
servants borrowed from other positions and, in addition, had
to recruit more than a hundred new personnel. These cadres
were trained in hamlet construction, organization of the people, and elementary intelligence techniques. They worked in
teams of six men each, mobilizing and supervising the manpower of the villages. The new recruits were paid with funds
provided in the U.S.-Vietnamese agreement, at the rate of
about 30 cents a day—just enough to cover living expenses.

We visited the area several times during the construction
phase. Army engineers were putting through the first road for
motor vehicles; they got fifty tons of cement from USOM
(through the Provincial Committee) to do the job. Through
the U.S. Military Assistance Program (MAP), barbed wire
and steel pickets for a double fence around each hamlet
were to have been provided. The people were to be compensated in a token way for their labor on the fences and moats.
Corvée labor, however outrageous it may seem in Western
eyes, has long been a tradition in Vietnam—a form of local
taxation to accomplish projects. Under the agreement, compensation was to be about a pound and a half of rice per man
day—equivalent to about 12 cents.

Civic-action teams and intelligence experts from the army
helped the village cadre teams set up information projects and
intelligence networks among the inhabitants. In the Commander's field headquarters, near the mouth of the coal mine
that was to supply the energy for the industrial complex, there
was elaborate provision for charts, pictures, and statistical ta-

bles to show the progress of the project, hamlet by hamlet. The number of families sympathetic to the Viet Cong or with former Vietminh adherents—particularly those whose sons went to the North in 1954—was noted, as well as the size and shape of the defense perimeter, the population, etc.

During the construction phase of the program, the area was well defended by regular army troops, and the Viet Cong could not get into the hamlets. Militiamen from the hamlets were recruited as volunteers and trained at division headquarters in Da Nang, two ten-man squads per hamlet. During the two-week training period, USOM paid the daily food costs and MAP provided ammunition and weapons.

In the most remote part of the valley, south of the coal mine, near the border with Quang Tin Province, efforts to pacify two hamlets were abandoned. When government troops came, most of the families fled to the mountains overhanging the hamlets. The few loyal families were relocated inside the defenses of two more secure hamlets closer to the coal mine.

As the construction phase was completed, the division began to withdraw the many troops that had been placed at strategic spots on hilltops overlooking the hamlets. The civic-action teams were removed, and the Province Chief took over the operation. There were still regular army soldiers at the industrial site in An Hoa, but their task was to protect only the site, not the citizens of the surrounding hamlets. There were also many special guards at the coal mine, paid by the government-owned mine company.

The defense of the population was left to a Civil Guard company (Regional Forces commanded by the Province Chief) and several squads of the Self-Defense Corps—now called Popular Forces—who covered an entire village, which usually included several hamlets. The volunteer militiamen were to protect only their own hamlet.

The province authorities had set up a training school for hamlet officials. For ten days, future hamlet leaders learned how to do their jobs and what resources the government had available for aid to their hamlets.

While the campaign was still under way in the An Hoa area, planning and training were in motion for the whole province. In three phases of three months each, the entire lowland area of the province was to be organized into strategic hamlets. The training program was also divided into three phases: 530 young men would be recruited and trained to work as village cadres; 9,000 militiamen would be trained for fourteen days; and 1,800 Hamlet Committeemen would get ten days of administrative training.

The An Hoa campaign was in high gear by January, 1963, and was scheduled to be completed by March. Operations elsewhere in the province were well under way by the end of April. All the cadres were in the field, and moats and other defenses —the outward signs of pacification—were appearing. Hundreds of militiamen and hamlet leaders were flowing to and from the training centers.

But the Province Chief had warned that the An Hoa operation was moving too quickly for proper and lasting results to be achieved, and that the program in the rest of the province would be slowed by the priority given to An Hoa.

Our field visits proved him right; we quickly turned up problems. At An Hoa, most of the people had not been paid for their work on the fences, and they were restless. The Province Chief claimed that the requisite papers had not yet been prepared, so he could not pay. He gave the same answer to complaints by families that they had not been compensated for the cost of relocating their homes (as they had been promised) inside the hamlet fences. Field checks showed that they had usually borrowed money to move and were paying 5 per cent interest monthly on the loans.

The barbed wire and pickets promised were not yet available. For the peasant, this meant that he would have to use his own bamboo, which had cash value to him. The hamlets constructed in 1962—before U.S. participation—cost each family $10 worth of bamboo (about one month's wages). The barbed wire and pickets finally came in giant quantities to Da Nang, but no provision had been made by U.S. MAP administrators for shipment out to the hamlets. It was repeatedly said that this was up to the Province Chief, who claimed he had neither enough trucks nor enough gasoline to do the job. After he had made many requests for trucks, the wire and pickets gradually began to move. But the delays were costly in terms of a coordinated hamlet-building schedule. Much of the barbed-wire transportation in 1963 was arranged by USOM with funds from the "miscellaneous" account.

By summer of 1963, several thousand militiamen had been trained and sent back to their hamlets. But many had no weapons. Faulty weapons maintenance and fear of losing U.S.-supplied carbines to the Viet Cong delayed the distribution. Only half the militiamen had a weapon they could use. Many of the fences they were trained to defend were only mounds of earth that lacked the promised barbed wire and pickets to deter the Viet Cong. The U.S. Military Sector Advisory Staff discovered several thousand rifles in a storehouse and got the Province Chief to begin repairs and distribution—eight months later. The Sector Adviser at the time was Major Douglas Christensen. His predecessor was Major Wayne McNulty. These advisers, as well as Major Milton Miller, the Civil Affairs Adviser, made a significant contribution to the pacification efforts in Quang Nam.

Security for the strategic hamlet was the primary, but not the only, goal of the campaign. Economic and social programs were also part of the effort. At the beginning of planning, the Vietnamese and the Americans had included projects that they thought would be popular among the rural people. These projects would be supplied as a form of compensation for the hard work and materials donated by the peasants in building the defenses. As soon as the hamlet was certified as "completed"—as having met the six-point national criteria—the economic and social benefits were to be available.

For the people of Quang Nam, schools are a matter of great importance. Education, as in the days of the mandarins, is a status symbol. In many villages, one can still find old men who can write Vietnamese in the Chinese characters—a system officially discarded several decades ago.

One of the general goals of the Strategic Hamlet Program was to have a school and a teacher in every hamlet. The Ministry of Education and the USOM Education Division had made an agreement to furnish the cost of a classroom (including cement donated through our logistics system), one year of salary for a teacher (including also costs for a two-month teacher-training program), and school supplies and textbooks. The hamlet had to furnish a volunteer to receive the training and serve as the teacher.

From among more than 200 hamlets "completed" in the first half of the year, the District Chiefs had made suggestions for 18 sites (totaling 42 classrooms) to the Provincial Education Chief. All schools had either 2 or 3 rooms and were built of concrete block or brick, with a tile roof. Rows of wooden desks and benches accommodated 50 to 70 students per school. The 42 school units authorized for 1963 had hardly scratched the surface of expressed need, and we soon began planning for a much larger school-construction program for 1964.

Perhaps the most far-reaching effort was the distribution of fertilizer to all farm families living in "completed" hamlets. the target was to give every farmer all the fertilizer he needed for up to about an acre of ground. But we did not have enough fertilizer to go around, so we limited the maximum to 44 lbs. —enough for about one-fourth of an acre.

Despite a complicated combination of three different kinds of fertilizer, we managed to get it delivered to the villages, with instructions for proper use. Most of the more than 50,000 farmers had never used chemical fertilizer before in their lives, but the results were excellent, and the response was almost incredible. As soon as the crop began to come up, the farmers were able to compare the greener, better rice plants on the fertilized lands with the plants on the rest of their fields and were impatient to extend the fertilizer to all their acreage. The Agriculture Chief of the province was jubilant, although from sample testing he had known well beforehand the probable results. He promptly asked for twice as much fertilizer for the next crop.

One of the great deficiencies in the diet of Quangnamese is protein. Most peasants feel lucky to get enough rice to eat, not to mention an occasional taste of meat. The Vietnamese Government and the USOM worked out a special program of pig-raising for poor families. The first effort was made in the densely populated coastal lowlands of Central Vietnam.

Each family permitted to participate would be given eight bags of cement to build a pig sty, using plans made by government experts. The National Agricultural Credit Organization would lend the farmer enough money to pay for improved breeds of pigs shipped from the Saigon area. He would be able to buy enough U.S. surplus corn to feed the pigs at a very low cost. The animal-husbandry service would provide free inoculations for the pigs and advise on better methods of pig-raising. The plan had a combination of worthwhile objectives: better diet, increased income, improved animal-raising, and an introduction to the use of agricultural credit.

Three different provincial bureaus had to cooperate to run the program, and it was a valuable new experience for the agricultural, animal-husbandry, and agricultural-credit technicians to work together. A joint Vietnamese-U.S. committee ran the province program, meeting monthly to chart plans and assess problems.

In theory, all the "floor plans" of the pig pens were the same, but Vietnamese artistic taste soared to unexpected

heights in some cases. One village offered a prize for the pret-
tiest pig pen. The winner was to get first choice from the batch
of pigs going to the farmers. A woman won, with a two-tone
brown-and-tan masterpiece that would have made a pig of any
pedigree blush with pride. Many of the pig pens shamed the
owner's home.

Assistance to the non-Vietnamese Highland peoples was a
special activity provided by USOM through the Provincial Rehabilitation Agreement. Highlanders would be resettled in secured areas, assisted in building houses, obtaining food and
medical care, construction of educational facilities, etc. Unfortunately the assistance came too late for the Katu tribe, the
only Highlanders in Quang Nam. The forty-three Katu who
chose not to go with the Viet Cong were living peacefully—but
in dire poverty—at An Diem, as noted earlier.

A joint Vietnamese-U.S. Special Forces camp was created
near An Diem in 1963 in the hope that the Katu could be
reached through the small settlement there. The Provincial
Committee, working through the nearby District Chief and
the Special Forces camp, financed relocation in new homes at
the Special Forces site, food allowances, a new school, and
even a special pig program.

The Highland ladies were quite proud of their pigs; they
kept the concrete floors of the sties spotless and cooked all the
food their pigs ate. After some pigs sickened, and even died, a
U.S. Army veterinary prescribed a shovelful of dirt in each pen
and uncooked food so they would get minerals and vitamins.
The pigs recovered.

Despite substantial efforts, more than a year of Special
Forces activity yielded no results in reaching more Katu. Pa-
trols would run across a few dwellings now and then, but the
inhabitants had always fled. In one carefully cultivated village
situation, they had left gifts and had hopes for eventual contact, but Vietnamese Air Force planes, considering the area a
"free" bombing zone, bombed the few dwellings out of exist-

ence a little later. The camp was disbanded in 1964 and the Highlanders were moved back to their previous location—which is now Viet Cong-controlled.

The delays in payments for house relocations and for construction of defenses at An Hoa continued. Some people had gone as long as eight months without being paid. A compromise method of paying the people at An Hoa was worked out: one-third of their debt was settled by payment in U.S. surplus wheat; the other two-thirds would be repaid with money, to avoid transportation problems that would arise if they were given rice, which they would have preferred. But the Province Chief continued to claim that he had no adequate forms to fill out on which to base payment (although we urged him to send extra clerks to speed it up).

By this time (September, 1963), Vietnamese and American official relations were severely strained over the Buddhist crisis. The very week that the Diem government raided the pagodas, the Province Chief finally issued (without our knowledge or consent) the funds to pay for the construction of the An Hoa defenses. A short time later, we were told that the Province Chief had delayed these payments in order to siphon most of the money into his own pockets, with the District Chief being forced to acquiesce in the scheme. Tension now reached a peak in our relations with the Province Chief.

When I arrived at Provincial Headquarters one day, I was denied access to the financial records that I had been examining the previous day. Twenty-four hours later, the officials showed me a completely new set of books (minus the embarrassing entries I had glimpsed the first day). At this point, in mid-October, 1963, I informed the Province Chief that I would not approve any further expenditures, pending investigation of indicated irregularities. Two weeks later, President Diem and his powerful brother were dead. The Province Chief was removed a week later—without penalty, unfortunately—and a new era in the life of the Republic had begun.

In many ways, the November coup brought a revolution to Quang Nam. The 1,800 students of Hoi An marched in celebration and would have proceeded with an embarrassing demonstration for the ouster of the Diemist Province Chief, had he not finally been removed from office. The repercussions extended even to me. While I was away, a gang of students appeared at the door of the house I lived in, prepared to ransack it. My landlord had apparently been one of the chief parties in government torture sessions, and his home had been almost torn to pieces. My cook pointed out the American sign on my door, and the students went away peacefully, expressing appreciation for American sympathy in the "revolution."

The political vacuum left by the demise of the Ngo family produced administrative paralysis in Quang Nam. The new Province Chief was a lieutenant colonel, with not a single day's experience in civil administration, who wanted to return to his troops. He was succeeded in a few weeks by a dynamic young colonel with administrative experience and considerable political ability.

Both Province Chiefs—and their subordinates—were fully cooperative and open to American suggestions. As the changes in personnel filtered down to lower levels, pacification efforts were eventually in the hands of entirely new people. Since the only high-level continuity was on the American side, we were forced to take a more leading role than we liked.

Nationally, the old "Strategic Hamlet" name was dropped in favor of a "New Life Hamlet" campaign. Forced relocation and other extreme measures were to be eased.

We were instructed by USOM in Saigon to encourage official actions that would create confidence among the people in the new government. The Provincial Committee arranged for immediate payment of six months' back salary for more than 200 health workers and the gift of 3 ambulances to district health centers. The ambulances were the first to be stationed in outlying districts. When the money and ambulances arrived, a public ceremony was made of distributing them. The Province Chief made a speech to the sizable crowd of health workers—mostly very young peasant girls—village notables, and plain villagers. He listened to many of the notables—who were dressed in the traditional black vestments over white pants, with black hats, beards, and Western umbrellas—as they spoke of their local problems and needs.

According to our planning timetable, our pacification effort was about six months behind. The Viet Cong had set us further back around the edges of the mountains by claiming responsibility for the coup and urging people to tear down their fences. A little later, they urged the people to refuse to use weapons because the Americans were purportedly running the new government as they had done in Diem's day. Government troops and police were not decisive enough in responding to these Viet Cong propaganda efforts, and sizable areas showed signs of a shift to confidence in the Viet Cong. Squads from seventeen hamlets in one district turned in their militia weapons and resigned. Many of these youth—well trained by Vietnamese Army instructors—are believed to have joined Viet Cong units.

Despite these events, most of the province was clear of overt Viet Cong activity. Our plan was to move as soon as possible into the development phase of hamlet activity, while consolidating the hamlets that needed strengthening. There were no funds left for hamlet-construction cadres; these had been expended before the coup, and no new funds had yet been authorized for 1964.

Before the corruption difficulties and the coup, plans had been laid for a vast economic and social development effort at the village level. The link between the government and the people in Quang Nam was to be a new economic cadre, more able, better trained, and better paid than the construction cadres. The idea was a local effort. No plans for carrying out village development had been worked out in Saigon on either the U.S. or the Vietnamese side. The province called for applicants with at least a ninth-grade education and a farm background. More than 600 applied for 120 positions. A written test was given (long a tradition in the Civil Service), and applicants who passed were interviewed in person by a panel.

The trainees received seventeen days of instruction in working with villagers and in the programs to be proposed. Specialists in agriculture, youth groups, education, construction, etc., taught these courses.

Each worker was sent to a village. He was assigned monthly emphases by a cadre-control committee, composed of the chiefs of relevant technical services. During the first month, the cadres were to inform the people about self-help projects and encourage requests. They were also to try to organize a young farmers' club among older youth no longer in school.

The cadres were not all well selected. Some were not serious, and others knew nothing about growing rice. A second recruiting effort was more successful. The recruiting team went into specific districts, hiring men from the district who were recommended by their village chiefs as good farmers. The age level went up, and the educational level went down.

In addition to the programs proposed in Saigon, the original national plan was to encourage local planning especially tailored to meet local needs. Before the coup, a U.S.-Vietnamese team had been scheduled to come from Saigon to review our province plans. In Quang Nam, we made our plans locally anyway, reporting to Saigon what we were doing.

Each of the technical-service chiefs was given a work sheet on which to list proposed projects his service would like to sponsor, noting money and materials requirements. These proposals, scores of them, were received and reviewed by a joint Government of Vietnam-U.S. committee. Most of the project proposals were discussed outside the formal meeting, and many of them were brought by the USOM Representative to Saigon for analysis by American and Vietnamese specialists.

We set up a budget, asked Saigon for the authorization and proceeded with what funds were already in the province. Saigon officials were still in the process of recovering from a second coup and its aftermath.

However, by mid-1964, USOM had sent an Assistant Provincial Representative to Quang Nam, along with a Filipino community-development expert. Also, two young specialists in agriculture and education were stationed by the International Voluntary Service (an AID contract group much like the Peace Corps, but established eight years earlier). These specialists worked closely with us and rendered valuable service.[1] Many other USOM specialists from Saigon assisted us via occasional visits to the province.

Major Warren Parker, on detached duty from U.S. Special Forces, was my assistant and successor. Tony Brillantes from the Philippines, and Tom Neal and Robert Biggers from IVS were moved out late in 1964 because of deteriorating security conditions. All gave great help in the program. Warren Parker and his assistant, Francis Savage, each received a Vietnamese medal for outstanding service during the flood emergency.

The province had made a good start in the hamlet program in 1963 by developing a special bureau to handle the campaign. With the advent of the development phase, the bureau was relocated and enlarged, and a higher-level bureau chief was brought in. A bilingual operations board charted the monthly allocations schedule of money and materials for each of more than 100 projects.

Forms to simplify and speed paperwork, and to improve information and control, were devised. A logistics section was set up to handle shipments to hamlets and from USOM warehouses in Da Nang. A fleet of a dozen World War II-vintage trucks had been secured from U.S. Army surplus and rebuilt. In addition, private contractors were hired to handle peak

[1] The first IVS death from enemy action occurred on November 12, 1965, when Peter Hunting, a Teamheader, was ambushed in a Delta province.

loads—forecast in advance by the requirements charted on the operations board. Six motor bikes were purchased to facilitate communications in truck deliveries and other field operations. The bikes were furnished to various technical services on loan whenever any service had a special program emphasis. Two warehouses were built, and a warehouse manager made a card inventory of each of scores of classifications, involving thousands of items.

A self-help section of the hamlet bureau dealt with more than 500 applications brought in from the field by village economic cadres. Special forms for particular self-help projects simplified processing; one form was designed for a school application, another for a well, a third for a road, etc.

The operation hardly compared to the sophistication of a modern Western data-processing system, and all its parts never did run right at the same time. But it was a great advance over the complicated methods used previously. Unfortunately, we were not able to bring the U.S. and Vietnamese reporting and financial systems together, so one set of receipts and one statistical reporting form never sufficed for both sides.

The greatest emphasis in economic efforts was on self-help. The village people chose a self-help project after meeting with the village worker. School construction was the most popular project. More than 200 units were authorized upon villagers' requests. The province supplied aluminum roofing, cement, and piasters; the people were to donate the rest. The chief problem was to induce the people to use the proper mixture of cement and sand. They nearly always tended to use too little cement.

Hundreds of wells were constructed. Some sandy areas needed large precast pipe to serve as well casings in order to avoid cave-ins. We built a precast yard and made a number of precast items to be taken by truck to the village projects.

In addition to self-help schools in Quang Nam, sixty units were financed in the second year by national programs.

Teacher-training classes were held, and salaries for one year were guaranteed. Salaries in these new schools were raised from $6 a month to $15 (which upset local payment rates).

At the textbook center in Saigon, hundreds of thousands of textbooks, beautifully designed and well written, went undistributed because there were no funds to transport them to the provinces. We got 14,000 books for Quang Nam only by flying them up by U.S. aircraft.

The 120 economic cadres spent most of their time in organizing agricultural improvement efforts; 64 young farmers' clubs were formed, and assistance projects were made available.

Ten credit unions were organized, and many more were requested. The province agricultural bank trained the participants to operate the unions, and it put up $500 cash as starting capital. The villagers put in their own money, and the result was doubly useful: more local capital available and more savings, as well.

Fruit trees—papaya, orange, mango, etc.—were distributed from a 40,000-tree nursery built especially for the purpose. Cuttings of improved varieties of sweet potatoes and many types of seeds not previously available to the province were also distributed.

As a conservation measure, 600,000 trees were planted on waste land. The people planted the trees and were paid 4 lbs. of bulgur wheat daily for their effort. Years later, these trees will supply firewood. For miles along the barren sand flats of the coastlands, about the only fuel now available are the pine needles and cones swept carefully from the hardy casuarina trees that thrive on pure beach sand.

Women were not overlooked in the economic and social programs, although Quang Nam had never had home-improvement workers before. Twenty female economic cadres were called in for special training by expert Vietnamese homemaker/teachers. After two weeks of intensive training in teaching sewing and other domestic skills, they were supplied with sixteen sewing machines and were sent out into three districts. Twenty women's clubs were formed. At their meetings, elementary, but new, methods of food preparation and preservation, sanitation, and child care were taught. After six successful months, this program was reduced to two girls because there was no national budget to "justify" it. Recently, however, approval from Saigon was given for nine of the girls to be reemployed in 1966.

The widely promoted Open-Arms surrender program, which sought to woo the Viet Cong back to the government side with promises for rehabilitation and assistance, had a hard time getting under way in Quang Nam. But eventually a steady stream of men, mostly very young and ill trained, came in and were housed and reoriented in a spirit of forgiveness and good will. A center to house the returnees was built adjoining a district demonstration center where crops were grown to prove their value to the community.

A 250-watt radio transmitter was secured from USOM in Saigon (like the trucks, also a rebuilt U.S. Army surplus item), and it became a highly effective channel of contact with most of the province. A studio was equipped, a staff hired and trained, and USIS personnel provided equipment and advice. USOM delivered individual radio receivers for sale to the peasants at low prices.

Drama teams for each district were trained to prepare and present propaganda-oriented shows in the hamlets. Village drama presentations are very popular and have long been an important tradition—one used effectively by the Viet Cong. In some places, our cadres were urged by the hamlet people to ask for more government drama teams, since they were regularly receiving performances at other times from the Viet Cong.

Hamlet movies were another popular program. Our target was to bring a movie to every hamlet every month. We never made it, but several movie teams regularly showed propaganda, educational, and entertainment films in the more secure areas. Inadequate equipment and maintenance were supplemented by excellent USIS assistance.

In cooperation with the youth service of the province, the village cadres organized volley-ball teams and arranged schedules for league play. Throughout the province, 376 teams were organized, and each was supplied with a net and a ball. The cost was low, for if replacements became necessary, they were to be made at the expense of the team members. The program was delayed by Saigon red tape for several months because there was no national program under which it could qualify for funds. Finally, persistent pressure from USOM in Saigon brought approval.

In evaluating the over-all effect of our security programs in Quang Nam, we must face some sobering facts. When province officials made a survey after the coup, they confirmed what we had suspected: thousands of families had been relocated without having been paid. Thousands more had been relocated without U.S. concurrence or funds to cover the cost. The Americans urged a crash program to pay the families—and tried to be present at the time of payment. But many families never got a penny. Changes of Province and District Chiefs and other officials had delayed and complicated the payment efforts. This must have been a major source of peasant discontent with the pacification program.

By the end of 1963, USOM had developed a widespread radio communications network, linking villages with districts and districts with Provincial Headquarters. This was intended to provide civil-defense warnings, as well as to serve administrative needs. Unfortunately the District Chiefs, who were responsible for the safety of the radios, would pull them into the district headquarters for fear of losing them to the Viet Cong. As a result, the network link was broken in the very situations where it was most needed.

Most of Quang Nam's population had been covered by 1963 with personal ID cards, but nothing had yet been done with the family-census-picture program. In 1964, we launched the program. Each family was photographed together, and its personal history was recorded. The picture was then mounted in the home so that police could check for any missing members.

For six months after the November, 1963, coup, there was little definitive leadership from the national level toward coordinated pacification policy. The Americans in Quang Nam pressed hard to begin pacifying a given area by using every resource at hand in proper sequence to complete the task. We supported the Province Chief, and those above him, who chose an area with strong Viet Cong control and personnel, about six miles west of the Da Nang air base. Known as the "four corners" area because four districts converge at that point, it was the vortex of Communist power in the lowlands.

The Vietnamese Army division in Da Nang assigned a regiment of troops to provide security, and the province police and technical services began working out the combination of political, economic, and social reforms thought applicable for a coordinated, thorough pacification effort. We knew it would take at least six months.

Within a few weeks, we were notified that the troops had withdrawn to go on a "special operation." They did not return. Viet Cong agents moved in and erased our efforts. A second time, troops were brought in to pacify, we cooperated, and the troops were abruptly withdrawn. After a third effort to pacify this area, we abandoned it completely. It will be a long time before those families friendly to the government forces will trust themselves to their protection again.

The Viet Cong steadily increased their numbers in the area west of Highway 1 and made a daring raid, in June, 1964, on the most populous hamlet on the highway between Da Nang and Hoi An. The headquarters was blown to bits, and fourteen militiamen were killed. No reinforcements were sent to relieve the militia, who held out for hours before succumbing.

From this time on, the Viet Cong presence was obvious throughout the province. Official travel, heretofore relatively free, was curtailed. By October, 1964, the Viet Cong were able to make the villagers on Highway 1 dig up more than 100 yards of the highway and mine it. My successor was caught in an ambush on the same stretch of road near Da Nang; he fortunately escaped unharmed.

In terms of pacification, Quang Nam's experience makes one theme quite clear. Successful pacification must be cautious, comprehensive, and coordinated. If troop support is not given over a long enough time, and without interruption, all the economic, social, and political efforts were wasted.

After I left Quang Nam, in August, 1964, three misfortunes hit the province in rapid succession: a devastating typhoon leveled many of our school projects; two months later, the worst flood in memory killed 3,000 people; and the Viet Cong established its control all the way to the shores of the China Sea, except for the areas around the district towns and provincial headquarters.

Another chapter in pacification efforts now is being written by more than 20,000 American Marines around Da Nang, in association with Vietnamese troops. A special zone for the rural area near Da Nang is beginning to receive constant protection and a comprehensive program of civic action. The Vietnamese and American civilian administrators and military officers are working together closely, but it is too early to assess the results of these efforts.

5

A SUMMING UP

THE EFFORT by the Vietnamese Government, with the cooperation of the American Office of Provincial Operations, to improve the lives of rural Vietnamese has unquestionably made progress, but it has been seriously limited in the past few years by three factors. First, Viet Cong terror, assassination, and attacks have hindered and made hazardous the execution of this program. The Viet Cong's military success has sharply reduced the areas in which this program can be administered. Until the security situation is radically improved, these rural efforts will be restricted and, therefore, have limited results. Second, the political instability in Saigon since November, 1963, has resulted in inadequate and ephemeral leadership and a lack of direction and guidance to lower officials. The constant changes in top personnel in the provinces have led to considerable inaction and undirected administration. Finally, partially because of the political and personnel difficulties, the governmental apparatus is inadequate and lacks trained and motivated officials to carry out any enlightened development and counterinsurgency programs that may be developed. The impact of these difficulties has not always been the same or constant, and consequently, the situation has varied in the different provinces and changed from time to time. However, at the risk of oversimplification and the danger of being rendered irrelevant by future changes, certain generalizations on progress can be made.[1]

In direct assistance to the Vietnamese military effort, the Provincial Rehabilitation Agreements provide support for local village defense forces (the Popular Forces) by giving these part-time soldiers per diem pay while they are in full-time training and thus unable to work, and long-term support for their families in the form of food, such as bulgur wheat and cooking oils. This assistance, carried out in close cooperation with the Vietnamese and American military, works well and has lightened the burden of part-time military service.

A more germane element of the provincial pacification effort is local development, which includes self-help projects and province-executed programs, but not major public works, which are administered from Saigon. Largely through imports of cement and tin roofing from the United States, there has been a general effort to provide the necessary buildings for schools, province and district offices, market places, and meeting rooms, which are expected to improve the general welfare of the people in the provinces. Additionally, specific projects have been undertaken to meet other local needs. In spite of the seeming abundance of water in Vietnam, potable water is in short supply in most places during at least parts of the year. In the Mekong Delta, the water is often brackish or subject to salt-water intrusions, while in the High Plateau, water is scarce in the dry season. One member of Provincial Operations, Robert Dunn, developed several new and different drilling rigs that seem faster and more efficient than the conventional ones. This small project, which involved only a very few Americans and Vietnamese, drilled a total of 120 wells during the six

---

[1] As Associate Director of USOM in charge of Provincial Operations, this writer made inspection tours of the provinces of Vietnam and had the opportunity of judging each provincial effort as well as of making over-all judgments.

months the program operated. Some were as deep as 700 feet. Also, cement was made available for many thousands of hand-dug wells. Another small project was the introduction of a simple brick-making machine that uses the local clay and can be run by unskilled workers. Hundreds of thousands, if not millions, of such bricks have been made in villages and hamlets and are used to construct houses, schools, and other public buildings. Inasmuch as lumber and stone are in short supply and most cement is imported, the ability to make local building materials has been an important gain for the people. Another attempt at modernization has been the introduction of windmills to lift water in the rice paddies; at present, water is transferred by hand, using small baskets. For technical reasons and because of cultural resistance to this innovation, the program has not gone well.

Provincial Operations has taken the lead and, with help from the Agricultural Division of United States Operations Mission, is advising and assisting the Ministry of Rural Affairs on three other programs. The first is the fertilizer and improved rice-seed program designed to increase rice production. This program started in Phu Yen Province and was promoted successfully by the Provincial Representative, Robert Burns. Before the recent Viet Cong inroads in that province, it was estimated that annual rice production had increased nearly 25 per cent. The program spread to other provinces, but at the moment, in many places the security situation has made continuation of the program difficult and an assessment of its results almost impossible. Where the program has gone forward free of Viet Cong activity, the results are excellent. A second program designed to improve the diet, especially in protein content, as well as provide some cash income for the peasants, is the pig-corn program. Under this project, a higher breed of hogs is being imported along with a better supply of food for them—corn. This program has gone well in many places. Many peasants understand the program, have increased their pig herds, and are beginning to derive an income from them. In other cases, the people have eaten the two or three pigs given them for breeding purposes or have eaten the corn. Another project, to provide local fish through the building and stocking of village ponds, again to improve the protein content of the diet, has been initiated in many provinces with good results. Had the security situation not worsened, there is little doubt that these measures would have greatly increased and improved the Vietnamese food supply and contributed to economic development..

With help from Provincial Operations and the Educational Division of the United States Operations Mission, the Vietnamese Ministry of Éducation is undertaking a major program of construction of elementary schools and a lesser one in the secondary field. In many cases, the school buildings were paid for and built by the government; in other cases, the people built the schools under a self-help program. Several thousand two-room and three-room school buildings have been constructed under this program. While the construction of the schools has gone quite well, in the matter of obtaining and training teachers, there has been less success. The salaries are low, almost below that for a private in the army, and teacher training has been inadequate and spotty. Sometimes, teachers have no sooner been trained than they have been drafted into the army. During the present emergency, some effort has been made to develop patriotism and loyalty to the government, largely by putting the national colors and patriotic slogans on textbooks and notebooks, but the results have been very limited. In this case, as in many others, more attention has been paid to the construction of buildings than to the teachers and curriculum that could make a real contribution to the community.

In the social-welfare field, Provincial Operations personnel, particularly Richard Evans, with the assistance of other divisions of the United States Operations Mission, have helped the Vietnamese Ministry of Social Welfare to handle the growing and complex refugee problem. This aid includes supplying blankets, food, and other necessities to provide temporarily at least for these unfortunate people. During the great flood of November, 1964, in the central lowlands, Provincial Operations coordinated the American efforts and worked closely with the Government of Vietnam in assisting the flood victims. A great amount of help and care has been provided, but the unpredictability of the size of the refugee influx, an inadequate administrative capability, and the security problem have overtaxed the resources allotted to this problem. Long-range planning for the refugees, numbering perhaps 400,000, is now beginning, and it is essential that careful provision be made for their care lest they become centers for Viet Cong activity.

A pilot women's program, under the supervision of Provincial Operations, was undertaken by Miss Kitty Hay in the Mekong Delta. After a month's survey to determine what the women were most concerned about, Miss Hay developed a one-week course providing instruction for Vietnamese women in improved agricultural methods, basic hygiene (especially midwifery), and reading and writing. Even more important, she wove into this course ideas on the role of women in a developing society and tried to stimulate the women to civic action. Traditionally, the women of Vietnam have done much of the work and played almost a dominant role in the family. Now, because large numbers of men are engaged in the war on one side or the other, women's roles and influence are perhaps even greater. By the fall of 1964, Miss Hay had begun to make real progress with women in the Delta, and there were plans for a small expansion. However, the program was cancelled by the Director of United States Operations Mission, and there is now no advisory program for rural Vietnamese women.

Another small effort assisted by Provincial Operations was a program for rehabilitation of disabled veterans so that they could become productive, self-supporting citizens. While a wide range of training was planned, the most active program was devoted to training veterans to become tailors. A Filipino, Pablo M. Quinto, who had had similar experience in the Philippines, was hired by Provincial Operations to advise on the rehabilitation program, but the Government of Vietnam, in the midst of a war, has not been very much interested in veterans' problems. Consequently, the results have not been outstanding. Recently, however, there have been indications of increased interest, and a better program may soon emerge.

The Chieu Hoi (Open-Arms) Program, potentially of great importance to the war effort, has had modest success. Charles Bohannan was one of the originators of the plan and its first adviser. John Perry of Provincial Operations followed him as the American adviser. Under Diem, this program was administered by a special bureau directly under the President's office. Since the November 1, 1963, revolution, the Chieu Hoi office —even more than other offices—has changed in rank and in organization many times. In the spring of 1965, it was made a separate ministry, but in the summer, it was reduced to an office in the Ministry of Psychological Warfare. The basic obstacle is that the Vietnamese really do not believe in the concept and cannot understand why defecting Viet Cong should be treated so well—perhaps even better than the average peasant. It is like the question explored in the Biblical story of the prodigal son: Why should one who has voluntarily left the fold be treated so well when he returns? Because of Vietnamese resistance to this idea, the national office in Saigon has seldom had top-flight leadership, has failed to provide adequate funds to the provinces, has been unimaginative in its appeals, and has not fulfilled promises made to the defectors. This situation in Saigon has not been conducive to aggressive provincial Chieu Hoi programs, but in spite of this, some provinces have had fairly good results. Since 1963, there have been more than 20,000 Viet Cong defectors, bringing perhaps 500 arms with them.

The purpose of the Chieu Hoi Program as initially outlined under the Diem government was to provide an opportunity for Viet Cong to defect without penalties for their previous actions. The program was not envisioned as an amnesty, but as a means for wayward members of the society to return to the government side and a normal life. The way a returnee or *rallié* (*quy chanh*, in Vietnamese) can demonstrate his faith is to bring his weapon to the government, to divulge intelligence information, and through interviews, to reveal his disillusionment with the Viet Cong. The returnees were to be well treated at all times and trained and otherwise helped to take their places in society as productive and loyal citizens.

The recent buildup of United States combat troops and increasing activity by the Vietnamese Army, and the stepped-up air activities of both nations, have harassed the Viet Cong, made their way of life even harsher, and necessitated constant movement. An imaginative and dynamic Chieu Hoi program—one that kept its promises—could play a vital role in this situation. Indications at this writing are that the United States will make a major effort to convince the Vietnamese of the necessity of making the Chieu Hoi Program effective and appealing.

This brief review of efforts by the Government of Vietnam, assisted by U.S. Provincial Operations, in the rural areas leads to several tentative general observations. Progress has been made in improving the material situation in certain social and economic fields and in many places. Numerous small public buildings have been constructed, more and purer water has been made available, local transportation facilities have been improved, and more and better food has been provided. Many refugees, some veterans and many *ralliés*, have been cared for. There is the beginning of a national elementary- and secondary-education system. Improvement has been made in the public health and medical fields. These are rather impressive achievements, given the underdeveloped nature of Vietnam and the rising Viet Cong threat.

The major objective of Provincial Operations, however, in seeking to help improve the material well-being of the people has been to assist the Government of Vietnam to gain the loyalty and active support of the people. How much these particular material efforts have contributed to developing a more loyal population is hard to say, and it is probably too early to make a meaningful judgment. Many of the people seem to be appreciative. Others of the population seem passive or unresponsive to these efforts, largely because they are much more concerned about security. Furthermore, reactions depend upon the way these efforts are presented to the people, the attitude of the local officials, and the extent to which they are responsive to the real needs of the people; thus they vary from province to province. At the present time, much of the population no longer has a free choice and even if the efforts of the Government of Vietnam, supported by Provincial Operations, have been partially successful, the gains have been more than offset by the Viet Cong terror campaign.[2]

There have been important and clear-cut contributions in other intangible areas, however. The Saigon Office of Provincial Operations and the Provincial Representatives have kept attention focused on the rural areas by their aggressive and continuous efforts. Saigon, in spite of some new interest in the countryside, easily slips back into its urban-biased ways and neglects the problems of the rural population. In Saigon, the Assistant Director of the United States Operations Mission and his staff, through close relations with the Vietnamese Pacification Committee, have been able to overcome many, but by no means all, of the roadblocks to effective action in the rural areas. Continued appeals by the Provincial Representa-

[2] However, the great present influx of refugees, as well as the recent increase in the number of defectors, may be evidence that the peasants object to Viet Cong methods and are beginning to prefer life under the government.

tives, who have daily administrative and logistics problems, have helped keep the pressure on.

The fact that in each province there are Provincial Representatives stationed for two-year tours, has provided an element of stability and continuity despite the political turmoil and numerous coups in Saigon. Province and District Chiefs have almost always changed after every coup, and the continued tension in Saigon has tended to make all of them fearful of taking action and insecure in their positions. Being new to the job and the province is also a handicap to the Province Chief —a handicap partially remedied by the knowledge and experience of the Provincial Representative in the province. However, the political instability in Saigon, though having an adverse effect on government in the provinces, has not been so damaging as one might expect. This writer was continually surprised during his visits to the provinces at how well the officials continued their planned efforts.

Through informal advice and discussion, the Provincial Representatives have had influence on the attitudes of some of the officials toward the population. Their drive and desire to get the job done have also motivated Vietnamese officials to action. The sense of service and dedication manifested by these Americans encouraged the Vietnamese officials in the same direction.

One significant and most moving testimonial to the efforts of Provincial Operations should be mentioned. It came, ironically, when Joseph Grainger, Provincial Representative in Phu Yen Province, was captured in July, 1964. The Viet Cong paraded him around the villages of the province and told the people that he was a dirty American imperialist. The villagers, with whom he had worked, defended him, even though they were under the Viet Cong gun, and said he was not a bad man. They said that he had come to their villages and helped them, and that they had seen him in the province with his children. They gave him food and drink, which he sorely needed. The Viet Cong realized that it was a mistake to exhibit him in Phu Yen Province, where he was known and liked, and they moved him out. Grainger was shot by the Viet Cong in January, 1965, while he was attempting to escape.

While some progress has been made in the fields of material improvement, in influencing the attitudes of officials, and in other areas of rural development, much remains to be done, and the program can and should be improved. Training programs and administrative procedures essential to carry out needed programs are still not adequate. The case of the Mobile Action Cadres illustrates some of the deficiencies. It was decided over two years ago that it would be useful to have trained, qualified mobile teams that could assist and supplement the village and hamlet governments in their pacification efforts. The members of the team were selected from the town population, not from villages or hamlets; they were not particularly qualified; and some were essentially political appointees. Instruction was poor and far too short, and efforts at motivation and attitudinal indoctrination were almost nil, so the teams were ill prepared for their job. They were no match for the Viet Cong cadres, who had often been trained for years and were well indoctrinated. Furthermore, because of vague instructions and loose administration and supervision, the teams sometimes competed with local officials rather than complementing them. Nor did it increase the stature of the local officials, or the respect or support of the people for them, when these newcomers brought extra money and materials that the local leaders had not been able to obtain. Though in a few cases the Mobile Action Cadres worked well, in most cases they were ineffective and merely one more layer of administrative red tape.

It has been suggested that Americans should help the Vietnamese develop proper and effective administrative procedures in Saigon and at the village level. Perhaps even more important, officials must be carefully selected, given some tenure, and trained and indoctrinated carefully and for longer periods of time. Local leadership, as well as national, should be aided and encouraged.

The major deficiency in the Government of Vietnam's rural program, and also in the Provincial Operations advisory effort, is that there has been a tendency to concentrate on the material aspects and to give only lip service to the intangible fields. Training and political indoctrination of personnel—teachers, government officials, or local leaders—has been poor and inadequate. Schools are built, but curriculum and teachers, students and parents are given little attention. A resources-control[3] program without adequately trained and motivated policemen will be useless and might even create additional unrest. No real effort has been made in the provinces to develop political institutions based on certain principles—or on any principles, for that matter. Calls for elections and generalized statements about the value of democracy are not adequate to fill the political vacuum in the provinces or in Saigon. Little or no effort has been made to help the Vietnamese develop their own viable social institutions, an essential process in a developing nation.[4]

There must be a greater effort to develop an ideology and a political base for Vietnam so that the nation's efforts have direction and meaning. Social institutions and organizations must be developed so that people can belong to their own society and participate in its development. It is critical that the people be organized so as to contribute to the counterinsurgency effort and to their own social, economic, and political development. People, not materials, hold the key to success in Vietnam.

Finally, there has been a tendency to haste in Vietnam and

[3] Resources control means limiting distribution and transportation of manpower as well as goods so that they do not reach the Viet Cong.

[4] The Lansdale team that Ambassador Lodge took with him on his return to Vietnam in August, 1965, has the mission of coping with these precise problems.

to insist on statistics even though they really do not reveal the true nature of progress or lack of it in political, social, and economic development. It is important to realize that the basic problems being dealt with cannot be solved quickly. People's loyalties and beliefs and actions do not change quickly, nor do their customs and social institutions. Thus, evaluations of certain programs cannot be made on a weekly or monthly basis. The Communists take years to build their hard core, and when they take less time and effort, the results are not good. The United States must not be impatient, but must gear its programs for a long and patient effort in the fields of human change.

The basic concept of Provincial Operations is sound. It has proved itself in many ways. The improvements suggested above, and others, can make it even better.

This experience of working at the lower echelons of government of another nation has highlighted some of the basic problems and dilemmas facing the United States in underdeveloped countries, particularly those threatened by or involved in insurgency. It also raises a few new ones. It is not the purpose of this book to examine these problems, but brief mention of them will be made as all arose in connection with Provincial Operations.

One specific problem raised by having Americans in the provinces is that of having two lines of communication between Saigon and the provinces—one American, one Vietnamese. This allows two routes to Saigon for complaints, queries, and administrative matters, and also two routes to the provinces for policy directives, administrative procedures, and general instructions. Though the United States Operations Mission effort is purely advisory, these dual communications can cause problems and misunderstandings. If the Government of Vietnam's instructions go out to its people first, without a simultaneous distribution to the American advisers, then the Americans do not know about or understand any new procedures or guidance and cannot advise or assist properly. If the English translation arrives in advance, it is even worse.

A more basic problem and one with no precise answer, is: How much can and should the United States do in an under-developed country? With a new and inexperienced government, with inadequate numbers of properly trained and oriented officials, progress is bound to be slow. If, as in the case of Vietnam, the country is involved in a serious insurgency, the problems are magnified and complicated, and the government cannot keep up with the promises of the insurgents or the expectations the insurgents generate in the people. This question of how much Americans should do becomes very specific at the lower echelons of government. There the question is not one of broad policy, such as whether an American should be the Minister of Economy; rather the question is whether an American should draw up the provincial program, deliver the cement, listen to grievances, and pay the people. In such situations, Americans frequently tend to want to take over and do the job themselves. At certain times and in certain circumstances, this may be feasible. In the vast majority of cases, however, it seems wiser and more productive in the long run for the Americans to take a back seat and to encourage, exhort, advise, and quietly assist the local officials. One of the goals of these rural efforts is to develop experienced, well-motivated officials. But this will never be achieved if the officials do not have a chance to learn by experience, to gain the respect of their own people, and to develop self-confidence and self-respect.

In Vietnam, another major question is whether the United States should encourage a decentralization of the government or insist on centralization at the Saigon level. There has been much discussion of this question, and strong views are held on both sides. The advantages of decentralization are that the local officials are more familiar with the situation, know the needs of the people better, and if given responsibility, can take the appropriate action more quickly and more effectively. Also, in an underdeveloped country, it is probably easier to grapple with local problems, which are simpler, than to try to do everything at the top, where the problems are more complicated and complex. This approach also gives flexibility; it permits officials to handle affairs in their own particular way, allows latitude for the different problems in various parts of the country, and encourages adjustment to a fast-moving situation during an insurgency. It helps develop leadership at the grass roots. On the other hand, centralization, theoretically at least, permits uniformity of policies and procedures and may counteract weak leadership in a given province. It also may develop capable officials at the higher levels of government, and such men will be badly needed as progress is made. Programs are also easier to control if power remains in one place.

Not only are there advantages and disadvantages on both sides of the question, but there is the question of degree: How much responsibility and power should be delegated, and to what level? At one time, there was considerable discussion of whether or not to delegate significant powers to the four corps commanders, so much power that there was concern that there might be four governments of Vietnam rather than one. Some Americans in Vietnam have contended that the district should be the key echelon in the rural program, while others believe that, since there are about 250 districts, this would result in too much diffusion of power and responsibility. Provincial Operations is based on the notion that the province is the key echelon and that considerable power and responsibility for local affairs should be delegated to the province. At the moment, a centralized governmental structure remains but with some delegation of authority to the provincial administrations.

In Provincial Operations, as well as in the Government of Vietnam, there was considerable discussion over how much of the effort should be made within the self-help framework. Many Provincial Representatives and Vietnamese felt that if its principles were understood and carried out properly, this procedure would be more conducive to committing the people to community development and giving them a stake in their village than if the government provided all things. For example, some Provincial Representatives argued strongly that the people like to build schools for their children, understand what they are, willingly help pay the teacher, and would defend the school against the Viet Cong. Other Provincial Representatives maintained that it was important that the government provide and staff schools as tangible evidence of its concern for the people; furthermore, this would provide a basis for a national public-education system. There seems to be a place for both systems in Vietnam today. One solution would be for the Saigon government to provide for national programs such as education, health, welfare, public works, etc., while allowing opportunities for the people to undertake local projects that they particularly desire through self-help.

Another dilemma faced in Vietnam, though less often now that the over-all situation has become extremely critical, is the allocation of effort between long-term projects and shorter-term, smaller-scale projects. Some Americans thought that major public-works projects and long-term economic-development measures were essential and should be pressed as much as possible, even with a poor security situation. Some projects, such as a water system for Saigon, a nationwide telephone network, and the highway systems, have been continued. Other Americans feel that smaller projects, which may have more immediate impact on the people, are necessary since the Viet Cong are exploiting underdevelopment in the rural areas. Some of both can be carried on, but there are in Vietnam, as we have seen, severe manpower and resource limitations on what can be done. In the present security situation, the major effort is devoted to short-term projects, though long-range, large-scale projects, such as port and harbor development, may be undertaken in the Cam Ranh Bay area.

A basic issue is whether and how much the United States should become involved in the social and political fields. While there seems to be little debate over United States assistance in education and health, there is much controversy over whether Americans can help build social institutions in Vietnam. Many argue that Vietnam is so different from America that we cannot possibly assist the Vietnamese in improving their existing institutions, much less help them in creating new ones. This writer would agree that we cannot do this job, but we can share our experiences and encourage institution-building, which is really the cement of a society. We can also share our political principles and ideals, as well as our experience in developing political institutions and governmental structures. The Vietnamese naturally are at liberty to accept or reject portions or even all of our experience, but if the United States commitment in Vietnam has any meaning, it is that we wish to share our political heritage with the Vietnamese and allow them the freedom to develop their own political and economic systems and social institutions. A corollary would be that we would hope, and perhaps even expect, that they will accept at least some of our principles, some aspects of our way of life, and not adopt the Communist way.

There is some debate as to whether it is desirable or possible to win the support of the people. The traditional argument, based on Communist doctrine, is that is it necessary to win the hearts and minds of the people. Another school of thought maintains that this goal is too ambitious and too long-range, and therefore should not be sought in insurgency situations.[5] These observers argue that it is the actions and behavior of the

[5] See Charles Wolf, Jr., "Insurgency and Counterinsurgency: New Myths and Old Realities" (unpublished RAND Paper). Much of the difference may hinge on the meaning or shade of meaning of the word "support." If it is interpreted to mean actions, there is little argument; if it is construed to mean loyalty, there is a difference.

people, not their loyalty, that must be influenced. They emphasize resources control, discipline, and the use of economic goods as rewards for the right behavior. Governmental actions should be considered in the light of how much they hurt the enemy, not whether they win the support of the people.

The difference may also reflect division over another question of whether it is best to supply an abundance of goods to the people and hope it gains their good will and good behavior, or whether there should be tight controls that can be used to deprive the enemy of goods and hurt his operations. There is an increasing amount of evidence, though the suspicion has long existed, that the Viet Cong in fact are acquiring a considerable portion of the supplies intended for the loyal population and for those sitting on the fence. There are indications that the Viet Cong have gained possession of much of the rice crop, inasmuch as Vietnam is now importing rice, whereas it had exported several hundred thousand tons two years ago. Through the use of fake companies and falsified customs receipts, the Viet Cong have gained possession of gasoline, medical supplies, and other materials. This economic subversion is a critical part of their covert operations to gain power. It would therefore seem that there is a need for an effective resources-control program in Vietnam and attempts are being made in that direction, but it will be hard to meet the requirement for highly trained personnel in fairly large numbers. Furthermore, in a country such as Vietnam, rich in food, a program of this kind is exceedingly difficult to carry out on a national basis. The United States Operations Mission is endeavoring to help the Government of Vietnam plan and execute a resources-control plan.

There are no precise answers to these questions and dilemmas, and the general answers will vary from time to time and place to place. The Provincial Operations program, however, was established on the basis of answers to certain of these problems. The underlying concept was that the Provincial

Representatives would act primarily as advisers with a view to helping develop a body of efficient and responsive Vietnamese officials. There was some compromise over how much Americans should do; the Provincial Representatives were granted money and materials which they were to control, but these were to be allocated by the Vietnamese Provincial Committees and put into the Vietnamese administrative system. Another decision was that in order to carry out a program in the rural area, a certain amount of decentralization was necessary. This was implemented through delegation of responsibilities and money to the province. A compromise was made on the issue of government-sponsored and self-help programs. There was a clear-cut decision that short-term projects were preferable to long-term projects in the present situation. Provincial Operations was committed to social and political action, but it has tended to concentrate on the material aspects of assistance. As the situation changes, the present answers may be modified.

A bonus stemming from the Provincial Operations effort is the discovery that there are many Americans who like to do this kind of work and do it well. The Provincial Representatives have demonstrated that Americans can advise at the grassroots level, under considerable pressure, and can get along with and help indigenous local officials. They have done what was asked of them and can also carry out many of the ideas for improvement of the rural program suggested in this chapter.

This Vietnamese experiment may have longer-term consequences of showing the way for more effective American help to countries that want and need it in their rural areas. There must, however, always be full agreement with the host government on such joint programs. There are indications that similar programs may be started in other countries. These efforts should start before active insurgency breaks out, and it should always be remembered that real progress will be slow and that the host country should do as much as it can on its own.

The commitment of substantial United States combat troops and air power to Vietnam during 1965 offers encouragement that the unfavorable military situation may be reversed and security gradually expanded. Recent events provide additional basis for this hope. Strange as it may seem, the military victory is the easiest part of the struggle. After this has been attained, the real challenge begins. If the combined United States–Government of Vietnam military effort does begin to re-establish security, another opportunity for nation-building in Vietnam will be gained. If this happens, there must be an effective effort to find and destroy the covert Viet Cong apparatus and to build a strong political structure in Saigon. If, concurrently, an improved rural program, as suggested earlier, is undertaken to help develop viable local government and a healthy socio-economic structure in the provinces, lasting peace can be achieved in Vietnam.

As this book goes to press, in February, 1966, President Johnson has just returned from his Honolulu meeting with Premier Ky and other South Vietnamese leaders. Together they reviewed the military and civil situations and programs. Particular attention was given to Premier Ky's intensified program of rural reconstruction, which is just getting under way. In their joint communiqué, issued as the Declaration of Honolulu, and in subsequent statements, President Johnson has given full U.S. support to this new civic-action program. It should be noted that similar high-sounding declarations in the past have accomplished little. However, with the full backing of the Saigon government and with such high-level American support, this new rural-development effort may succeed.

INDEX